ABC's for Coaching Yourself to Success

HOW TO ID YOUR INTERNAL DRIVER AND WHY IT MATTERS

Awareness, Behaviors, and Connections

Jennifer Chloupek, M.Ed.

DocUmeant *Publishing*
244 5th Avenue
Suite G-200
NY, NY 10001
646-233-4366
www.DocUmeantPublishing.com

Copyright © 2023 All rights reserved. Chloupek Consulting Services

Published by
DocUmeant Publishing
244 5th Avenue, Suite G-200
NY, NY 10001
646–233-4366

Limit of Liability and Disclaimer of Warranty: The publisher has used its best efforts in preparing this book and the information provided herein is provided "as is.

No part of this book may be reproduced or transmitted in any form or by any means, electronic or mechanical, including photocopying, recording or by any information storage or retrieval system, except as may be expressly permitted by law or in writing from the publisher, or except by a reviewer who may quote brief passages in review to be printed in a magazine, newspaper, or online website.

Permission should be addressed in writing to:
publisher@DocUmeantPublishing.com

Cover Design & Format by Ginger Marks

Edited by Philip S. Marks

Illustrations and layout by DocUmeant Designs
www.DocUmeantDesigns.com

Library of Congress Cataloging-in-Publication Data

Names: Chloupek, Jennifer, author.
Title: How to ID your internal driver and why it matters : awareness, behaviors and connections / Jennifer Chloupek, M.Ed. ; [edited by] Philip S. Marks, Ginger Marks.
Description: NY, NY : DocUmeant Publishing, [2023] | Series: Core connections awareness series; Vol 2 | At head of title: ABC's for Coaching Yourself to Success. | Summary: "How To ID Your Internal Driver and Why It Matters takes readers on a transformative journey of self-exploration, helping them unveil their internal drivers through a unique workbook format. Through reflective exercises and thought-provoking prompts, this interactive guide facilitates a deep understanding of how past experiences have shaped personal values, while encouraging an exploration of present behaviors and connections. By fostering self-awareness, aligning behaviors with core motivations, and evaluating relationships, readers gain the tools to lead a more authentic and purpose-driven life"-- Provided by publisher.
Identifiers: LCCN 2023037888 | ISBN 9781957832098 (paperback)
Subjects: LCSH: Motivation (Psychology) | Self-consciousness (Awareness) | Self-perception. | Self-actualization (Psychology)
Classification: LCC BF503 .C56 2023 | DDC 153.8--dc23/eng/20230927
LC record available at https://lccn.loc.gov/2023037888

CONTENTS

Introduction	1
PART One: Examine CORE-Awareness	5
PART Two: Evidence CORE Behaviors	53
PART Three: Engagement CORE Connections	87
PART Four: Explore Case Studies	103
ID Reflections / Notes	135
About the Author	157

"The journey of a thousand miles begins with one step."

—Lao Tzu

INTRODUCTION

Your (ID), or the identification of the force or motivation that drives you, can serve as a powerful tool in navigating through life. By understanding your ID, you gain clarity of your awareness, behaviors, connections, passions, and priorities. This may help you make more informed decisions, set appropriate goals, and stay focused on what truly matters to you.

Think of your *Internal Driver (ID)* as your driver's license. It gives you permission to steer your own course and make choices that align with your values and aspirations. When you know what drives you, you can take ownership of your life and create a road-map that reflects your unique vision and goals. This can give you a sense of empowerment, even in the face of challenges and setbacks.

Your ID can help you stay true to yourself and avoid getting sidetracked by external pressures or expectations. When you know what you stand for, you can resist the temptation to conform or compromise your values to fit in or please others. This can foster a sense of authenticity and integrity, which can, in turn, attract like-minded individuals and opportunities that align with your ID.

Your ID can be a powerful tool for self-discovery and growth. By exploring and nurturing your ID, you can unlock your full potential, live a more purposeful life, and make a positive impact on the world.

In this book you will focus on three parts: *Awareness*, *Behaviors*, and *Connections*. This is the true ABC's for your personal and professional success.

When you put in the hard work and identify your ID, your navigation will become clearer and the view from the rear-view mirror will begin to come together too. This will steer you to success.

As executive coaches, we have studied the matter of motivation. We can help you figure out why you do what you do. The motives, the reasons, and the things that drive you have a name, your "Internal Driver". It represents what drives you and can be distilled into a word or a phrase that represents you, describes you, and connects you to you.

Living in today's fast-paced world, have you ever slowed down long enough to pause and think about why you do the things you do? What makes you act a certain way? What motivates you when you wake up in the morning and what keeps you going until you put your head down on your pillow at night? Your life seems to run on autopilot. You can become increasingly unaware of why you act, behave, or respond the way you do.

The goal of this book is to help you slow down long enough to take this journey of self-discovery. It will help you become fully aware of what drives you and to celebrate your individual uniqueness by becoming fully aware of your ID.

Before you answer these questions, you need to take a short peak into the behavioral sciences to explore the concept of internal motivation. During the early 20th century, scientists believed human beings were driven by their biological urges.

Mid-20th century, seminal researchers in behavioral sciences discovered that not only are people driven by their biological urges, but they also respond to Rewards and Punishments. This second drive became prominent in the work environment and served as external motivation for rewarding – and reprimanding – employees.

Over the last several decades, scientists have focused on what they believe is a third drive, Internal Motivation. This internal motivation that drives people can be harnessed and used to help companies figure out what determines employees' behaviors, and what might account for the way in which they interact and communicate with others.

Moving forward, we will refer to this internal motivation as your ID. You may or may not know or have labeled your ID, but after reading this book you will have a better understanding of what your ID is, and how it can be used to benefit all, and how it can potentially be used in a way that is not working for you and others.

According to the United States Census Bureau, the world population has reached seven billion—and is still climbing. When you begin to think about that number with regards to those living and contemplate the fact that every one of us is uniquely made, it makes you wonder why people behave or operate in the way in which they do.

It is an amazing fact that humans are comprised of many of the same elements, but even though we (humans) have many similarities, we are all vastly different, in most areas.

Your focus is to narrow that broad scope of how you are similar, and to celebrate your differences and what drives you to behave the way you do. Most importantly, you will focus on what drives you to behave the way you do in the work environment. You will become aware of how this can impact the way you communicate, achieve results, and respond to demands that face you every day.

Before you can embark on your exploration of your very own personal ID, there are a couple of things that first need to be discovered or re-discovered. Please join us on this journey as you make your exploration to find your ID.

***

This book is divided into 3 parts. The ABC's for Coaching Yourself to Success.

"A" stands for Awareness, "B" stands for Behaviors, and "C" stands for Connections. The word Core is placed in front of each word to represent you. You are the Core of your story. The purpose of this book is to gain knowledge around your Core-Awareness, Core-Behaviors, and Core-Connections. By gaining this knowledge you will be more successful in all areas of your life. This book is designed to help coach you through all stages of your life and can help you both personally and professionally.

Part 1 we call Core-Awareness. This is the EXAMINE portion of the book. You will examine different points in your journey to discover your ID. This discovery will give you insight into your behavior and why you do what you do. Everyone has a unique ID that is made up of their personal story and experiences.

After discovering your ID you will have the opportunity to complete other assessments and activities that will give you a greater Core-Awareness.

Part 2 we call Core-Behaviors. This is the EVIDENCE portion of the book. You will see how your behaviors are unique to your ID. You will identify how your behaviors are working for you—and possibly working against you according to your ID.

You will have the opportunity to complete activities and tools to help coach yourself along your journey.

Part 3 we call Core-Connections. This is the ENGAGEMENT portion of the book. You will begin to make connections on how your ID plays into the relationships that you have both personally and professionally. You will also begin to understand how others have their own ID.

Part 4 we call Case Studies. This is the EXPLORE portion of the book. You will begin to pull together your ID and examine it from a case study perspective. You will explore the good, the bad, and the ugly as it relates to your own ID.

The activities and tools in this part will help you with relationships by connecting with others and learning how to appreciate the uniqueness of those you encounter.

PART ONE: EXAMINE
CORE-AWARENESS

> "Not all those who wander are lost."
>
> —J.R.R. Tolkien

CORE-AWARENESS

CULTIVATING CORE-AWARENESS INVOLVES a deeper sense of self-awareness and becoming more attuned to your thoughts, emotions, and behaviors. It is a transformative journey that requires a commitment to self-reflection and mindfulness. Here are a few steps that you may want to pay attention to, and become more conscious of, while gaining core-awareness.

You can start by practicing mindfulness meditation. This involves paying attention to the present moment, observing your thoughts and emotions without judgment, and cultivating a sense of inner peace and stillness. Mindfulness meditation can help you become more aware of your internal world, allowing you to gain a deeper understanding of your thoughts, emotions, and behaviors.

You can also engage in self-reflection activities, such as journaling or introspection. These activities can help you explore your inner world and gain insights into your Core-Awareness. You can ask yourself questions such as "What are my strengths and weaknesses?" or "What are my core values?" to gain a deeper understanding of yourself.

You can also seek feedback from others who know you well. Sometimes, others can offer insights into your behavior and patterns that you may not have noticed yourself, allowing you to gain a broader perspective of your core-awareness.

Becoming more conscious of your core-awareness takes time and commitment to self-reflection and mindfulness. By practicing *mindfulness meditation, engaging in self-reflection activities, and seeking feedback from others*, you can become more attuned to your thoughts, emotions, and behaviors, allowing you to cultivate a deeper sense of core-awareness.

Discover Your Internal Driver

Discovering your ID can be a challenging task as it requires a deep understanding of your inner self and the factors that drive you. There are a few steps that you can take to help you identify your ID.

Start by reflecting on your past experiences and identifying the moments where you felt the most fulfilled and accomplished. These experiences may provide clues as to what motivates you and what drives your passion.

You can also examine and consider your values and beliefs. Your ID is often rooted in your core values and beliefs, and understanding what these are can help you identify what truly matters to you. You can ask yourself questions such as "What do I stand for?" or "What are my priorities in life?" to gain a deeper understanding of your values and beliefs.

Seeking feedback from friends who know you well can also help you find your ID. Sometimes, others can offer insights that you may not have considered, and their feedback may help you gain a different perspective on what motivates you.

Discovering your ID takes time and self-reflection, but by considering your past experiences, values and beliefs, strengths and weaknesses, passions and seeking feedback from others, you can gain a clearer understanding of what drives you, what you are passionate about, and what goals would be most appropriate for you.

The discovery of your ID will give you deeper insights into your Core-Awareness.

Let's provide a basic framework and common definition of your "Internal Driver". Your ID is a fundamental driving force or underlying reason that inspires and fuels your actions and behaviors. It is the deep-seated desire or need that compels you to pursue a particular goal or objective. Your ID is intrinsic, meaning it comes from within you, can be manifested externally, and seen by others.

In many cases, a person's ID is closely tied to their values and beliefs. For example, someone who is motivated by a desire to help others may have values such as empathy and compassion that drive this motivation. Similarly, someone who is motivated by a desire for financial success may have values such as ambition and perseverance that support this drive.

Understanding your ID can be an essential step in setting and achieving goals, as it helps to clarify why certain goals are more desirable and important to you and how they align with your core values and beliefs. By identifying your ID, you can better understand what drives you and how to channel that motivation into productive actions that help you achieve your objectives.

To discover your ID, you will start by EXAMINING two areas: **The Past and the Present**. During your examination of the past, you will look at the people, places, and values/beliefs that you can recall that add to your story and shape how you view and experience the world. All these experiences are your filters.

During your examination of the present, you will look at your strengths, weaknesses, and where you derive your energy and passion. You will also ask for feedback from others to gain valuable insights.

Before embarking on this journey, let's look at a few Internal Driver phrases that my clients have come up with that may help you better understand the concept.

Your goal is to come up with your unique ID phrase based on your *past and present experiences*. There are so many computerized assessments out there that try to capture your tendencies and behaviors, however they don't examine your story. This is the opportunity to bring your life data to the pages of this book to determine your unique ID phrase.

Your story matters and what it tells matters. Your ID is where and how you spend your time, energy, and effort. Your ID represents what drives you and can be distilled into a phrase that represents you. On the following page are some Internal Driver Phrase examples to help you identify your personal ID.

Internal Driver Phrase Examples

To never give up.

To never take no for an answer.

To persevere through all challenges.

To put in the extra effort.

To prove my worth.

To police.

To get it right.

To get it done.

To rise above all obstacles.

To be heard.

To make your voice count.

To speak up.

To be assertive and confident.

To express myself clearly and concisely.

To make sure I am heard.

To be the best.

To aim high and never settle.

To be the best at everything I do.

To constantly strive to improve.

To raise the bar for myself and others.

To never settle for second best.

To disrupt.

To break the mold.

To think outside the box.

To constantly innovate.

To discover new and revolutionary ideas.

To belong.

Past Experiences – EXAMINE

Your past experiences can have a significant impact on your ID, which is the fundamental driver of your behavior. These motivators are shaped by your values, beliefs, and goals, which are often influenced by your past experiences.

Someone who experienced financial hardship as a child may be motivated to pursue financial stability and success as an adult. This motivation may stem from a desire to avoid the stress and uncertainty of financial instability, and to provide a better life for themselves and their loved ones. Their ID phrase could be: to be successful, or to achieve important goals. Similarly, someone who experienced rejection or social isolation in the past may be motivated to seek out social connection and acceptance. This motivation may be driven by a desire to overcome the pain and loneliness of their past, and to find a sense of belonging and community in their present life. Their Internal Driver phrase could be "to belong and be accepted."

Past experiences can also shape your beliefs and values, which in turn influence your ID. For example, someone who experienced discrimination or injustice in the past may hold values of equality and social justice, which can motivate them to pursue activism and advocacy in their adult life. Their ID phrase could be: "To speak up and have a voice."

Past experiences play a crucial role in shaping your ID by influencing your values, beliefs, and goals. By reflecting on your past experiences and understanding how they have shaped your motivations, you can gain greater insight into your own behavior and work towards achieving your goals in a way that is authentic and fulfilling.

Are you ready to begin the journey and take a detour to the past? Let's go!

PAST EXPERIENCES: EXAMINE – PEOPLE, PLACES, VALUES, AND BELIEFS

The people from your past, such as your parents, caregivers, mentors, friends, enemies, and peers, can all have a lasting impact on your ID. Your relationships with these individuals have shaped your beliefs about yourself and others and influenced your behaviors, connections, goals, and aspirations.

Someone who grew up with supportive and encouraging parents may be motivated to pursue their passions and develop their skills, while someone who experienced neglect or abuse may struggle with self-esteem and motivation.

The places you lived and the values and beliefs you internalized from your past can also shape your ID. Your physical surroundings, such as your childhood home or neighborhood, have shaped your experiences, perspectives, and sense of identity, which, in turn, influence your behaviors, connections, goals, and aspirations. Similarly, the values and beliefs you internalized from your family, culture, or community have shaped your worldview and influenced your behaviors, connections, goals, and aspirations.

The people, places, values, and beliefs from your past can have a significant impact on your ID, shaping your values, beliefs, and goals, and influencing the direction of your life.

By becoming aware of these influences and reflecting on your own experiences and perspectives, you can gain greater insight into your ID and work towards achieving your goals in a way that is authentic and fulfilling.

Who were the people from your formative years who influenced you?

_____

_____

_____

_____

What places during your formative years shaped and influenced you?

_____

_____

_____

_____

What were the messages that you learned from others?

_____

_____

_____

_____

How many siblings do you have and where were you in the birth order?

What were you like in school?

What were you known for in your early years?

Values and Beliefs

Your values and beliefs are also key factors in shaping your ID. Your fundamental principles and beliefs about yourself, others, and the world around you can influence your goals and aspirations. They can motivate you to pursue certain actions and behaviors. Someone who values personal achievement and success may be motivated to pursue an administrative or political career. Their ID Phrase could be "To accumulate power while having control."

Core-Beliefs

The beliefs that you learned in your formative years can significantly shape your actions and behaviors as an adult. This includes a substantial number of people (e.g., the media) from whom you will develop strong opinions but will never actually meet in person. During childhood, you absorb and internalize beliefs about yourself, others, and the world around you. These beliefs become part of your subconscious mind and can influence your thoughts, emotions, and behaviors throughout your life.

For example, if a child grows up in an environment where they are constantly told that they are not good enough or that they cannot achieve their goals, they may internalize these beliefs and struggle with low self-esteem and a lack of confidence as an adult. On the other hand, if a child is encouraged to pursue their interests and is praised for their efforts, they may develop a sense of confidence and a belief in their ability to achieve their goals.

The beliefs that you learn from others, and the world, can also shape your actions and behaviors as adults. For example, if a child is warned not to venture into a high crime neighborhood and observes that her mother and her friends don't go there themselves then the child probably assumes there is a serious reason for that. If a child grows up in an environment where they are taught to fear people who are different from them, they may struggle with prejudice and discrimination as an adult. Conversely, if a child is taught to value diversity and respect others, they may be more open-minded and inclusive in their interactions with others as an adult.

The beliefs that you learn in your formative years can have a lasting impact on your actions and behaviors as an adult, shaping the way you think, feel, and interact with the world around you.

What beliefs did you hear from others that you carried forward with you today?

What beliefs did you hear about yourself?

Where do you see these beliefs in your life today?

Are these beliefs true and how do you know?

What might you keep and what might you let go?

Beliefs Assessment

Below is a series of statements about beliefs. Read each statement and rate how much you agree or disagree with it on a scale of 1 to 5, where 1 means strongly disagree and 5 means strongly agree. There are no right or wrong answers, so please answer each question honestly and to the best of your ability.

I believe that beliefs are essential to living a fulfilling life. ....

I believe that your beliefs are shaped by your upbringing and life experiences. ....

I believe that it is important to regularly examine and reevaluate your beliefs. ....

I believe that beliefs can be changed with evidence and new information. ....

I believe that it is important to respect other people's beliefs, even if you don't agree with them. ....

I believe that some beliefs are harmful and should be actively challenged. ....

I believe that beliefs can sometimes be irrational and unsupported by evidence. ....

I believe that it is important to have a balance between holding onto your beliefs and being open to new perspectives. ....

I believe that your beliefs can influence your behavior and decision-making. ....

I believe that it is important to have a diverse range of beliefs in society. ....

Scoring:

Add up your scores for each question. Higher scores indicate a greater degree of belief in the importance and influence of beliefs.

INTERPRETATION:
10-20: You may have a more skeptical or apathetic attitude towards beliefs.
20-30: You recognize the importance of beliefs but may not actively engage in examining or reevaluating them.
30-40: You have a strong belief in the importance and influence of beliefs but may also recognize the need for balance and respect for diverse perspectives.
40-50: Your beliefs play a significant role in your life and decision-making, and you regularly examine and challenge them in order to grow and learn.

What did you learn from the above Belief's Assessment?

What do you plan on doing with this data?

What have you learned that might shape your ID?

I know you are just starting this journey, however, are any phrases surfacing with you? If so, write them below. Your job is to collect as much data about you to better understand you!

CORE VALUES

Your core values and your ID are closely intertwined, as your values often shape your behaviors, connections, goals, and aspirations, which in turn motivate you to pursue certain actions and behaviors. Core values refer to the fundamental principles and beliefs that you hold about yourself, others, and the world around you. These values can include concepts such as honesty, integrity, compassion, respect, and justice.

Your core values began to take shape in your formative years. You explore your values in the Past Experiences part of this book because your values were beginning to become ingrained at that point.

Your core values are the principles and standards that are unique and intrinsic to you, and they most often show up in the way that you behave.

Your core values are a piece of the puzzle that helps you to unlock and discover your ID. They come into play when you communicate, act, react, or respond.

Your ID is the fundamental driver of your behavior and is often linked to your core values. For example, if someone highly values creativity and self-expression, they may be motivated to pursue a career or hobby that allows them to express themselves creatively. Their ID could guide them to be creative and expressive. Similarly, someone who values helping others may be motivated to pursue a career in healthcare or social work. Their ID Phrase could be: "To serve" or "To help".

Understanding your core values and how they relate to your ID can help you gain insight into your own behavior and work toward achieving your goals in a way that is authentic and fulfilling. By aligning your ID with your core values, you can create a sense of coherence and purpose in your life and live in a way that is true to yourself and your deepest beliefs.

Assessment for Identifying Core Values

In this assessment, you will be presented with a series of statements. Read each statement and decide how much you agree with it on a scale of 1 to 5, where 1 means strongly disagree and 5 means strongly agree. Choose the number that best represents your level of agreement with each statement.

.... I believe that honesty is always the best policy, even if it is difficult or uncomfortable to tell the truth.

.... I value spending time with my family and close friends over other activities.

.... I believe in treating everyone with respect, regardless of their background or beliefs.

.... I feel fulfilled when I am able to help others and make a positive impact on their lives.

.... I believe in taking responsibility for my own actions and decisions.

.... I prioritize continuous learning and growth and enjoy trying new things and taking on challenges.

.... I believe in working hard and putting in effort to achieve my goals.

.... I prioritize my own well-being and self-care and believe in taking care of my physical and mental health.

.... I value creativity and self-expression and enjoy exploring new ideas and experiences.

.... I believe in being environmentally conscious and taking steps to protect the planet.

Scoring:

Add up your scores for each statement and rank the statements in order of importance based on your total score. The statements with the highest scores are likely to be your core values.

Interpreting Your Results:

Your core values are the beliefs and principles that guide your life and decision-making. They represent what you stand for, and what you believe is important. By identifying your core values, you can gain a greater understanding of yourself and what motivates you and can use this knowledge to make better decisions and live a more fulfilling life. Use your results to reflect on what matters most to you and consider how you can align your actions with your core values.

If you have identified that your number one value is Balance and you work at a job that demands you to work around the clock, how might this play out in your behavior?

_____
_____
_____
_____

Are you beginning to see a theme on what drives and motivates you to do what you do? If so, write your thoughts below:

_____
_____
_____

Exercise: EXAMINE – PAST EXPERIENCES Core Values

We all value different things. Understanding what you value the most helps you better understand your motivations, behaviors and ultimately your ID.

From the list below pick your top 3 values:

Integrity	Compassion	Loyalty
Honesty	Responsibility	Open-mindedness
Accountability	Kindness	Creativity
Respect	Fairness	Authenticity
Empathy	Trust	Perseverance

ABC's for Success: Awareness, Behaviors, Connections

Courage	Tolerance	Diversity
Generosity	Self-awareness	Innovation
Gratitude	Self-improvement	Excellence
Patience	Teamwork	Discipline
Humility	Collaboration	

What are your top 3 values?

_____

_____

_____

How did you determine your top 3 values?

_____

_____

_____

_____

What do your top 3 values tell you about yourself?

_____

_____

_____

_____

Are you able to live out these values in your personal and professional life?

What happens when you can't live out these values?

Where do my values align with what I am doing?

Where and when are my values challenged?

Do you have competing values? If so, what can you do?

Tying it All Together: EXAMINE – PAST EXPERIENCES Understanding Your ID

Answer the following questions honestly to gain a deeper understanding of how people, places, values, and beliefs create your ID.

People: Who are the people in your life that have had the greatest influence on you? This could be family, friends, mentors, or anyone else who has had a significant impact on your life. How have they influenced you?

Places: What places have had the greatest impact on you? This could be a childhood home, a favorite vacation spot, or any other location that holds special meaning for you. How have these places impacted your values and beliefs?

Core-Values: What are your most important values? These could be things like honesty, integrity, kindness, or creativity. Why are these values important to you?

....

....

....

....

Beliefs: What are your beliefs about the world and your place in it? Do you believe in a higher power, a purpose for your life, or a certain way of living? How do these beliefs motivate you?

....

....

....

....

Internal Driver: Based on your answers to the previous questions, what do you think might be your ID? In other words, what drives you to do the things you do and be the person you are? How do your people, places, values, and beliefs contribute to this motivator?

....

....

....

....

Present State: EXAMINE – Strengths, Weaknesses, Energy, Passion, Feedback

Diving into your Past Experiences should have given you great insight to begin to discover your ID. Your Past Experiences have been one piece of data that you have EXAMINED, you still have some ground to cover to EXAMINE during this journey. We will now look at your Present State.

The areas you will EXAMINE during your Present State are your strengths, weaknesses, energy, passion, and feedback. By EXAMINING these areas, you can begin to recognize your ID. Understanding these areas can help you identify what drives you, what challenges you, and what keeps you engaged and fulfilled.

Look for patterns in your life that highlight your ID. Examine recurring themes, interests, or goals that have remained consistent.

By tying together your Past Experiences and your Present State, you will ultimately discover your ID. This discovery is one data point in becoming more core-aware, which is your end goal.

Strengths are the qualities and skills that come naturally to you, which you can use to excel in your work and personal life. When your strengths align with your interests and values, it can boost your confidence and motivation. On the other hand, weaknesses can create self-doubt and hinder progress, making it important to identify and address them.

Energy and passion are closely linked to motivation. A person who is energized by their work is more likely to feel motivated to tackle challenges and persevere through difficult times. Passion is also a powerful motivator, as it drives individuals to pursue their interests and goals with enthusiasm and dedication.

Feedback is another essential factor that shapes your ID. Constructive feedback can help you identify areas for improvement and gain a better understanding of your strengths and weaknesses. Positive feedback can also boost motivation by providing a sense of accomplishment and recognition.

Your Present State plays a critical role in shaping your ID. Understanding your strengths, weaknesses, energy, passion, and feedback can help you identify your ID.

You are now ready to begin the second part of your journey, let's go!

Strengths and Weaknesses

Discovering your strengths and weaknesses is an essential step towards identifying your ID. Your ID is the driving force that propels you forward and gives you a sense of purpose and fulfillment. By understanding your strengths and weaknesses, you can identify the areas where you are naturally talented and passionate, as well as the areas where you may need to work on and develop.

The following are some steps you can take to discover your strengths and weaknesses:

Take a personality test: There are many online personality tests available that can help you identify your strengths and weaknesses. These tests are designed to assess your personality traits, values, and interests, and can provide valuable insights into your natural abilities and inclinations.

Ask for feedback: Ask friends, family members, and colleagues for feedback on your strengths and weaknesses. This can be a helpful way to gain a different perspective on your skills and abilities and can provide insights that you may not have considered before. Sometimes by asking for feedback around what you can start doing, stop doing, and continue to do can help you identify strengths and weaknesses.

Reflect on your past successes and failures: Think about times when you have excelled and achieved success, as well as times when you have faced challenges or setbacks. Consider what skills and strengths you utilized to achieve success, and what weaknesses may have contributed to your struggles.

Experiment with new activities: Trying new activities can be a great way to discover your strengths and weaknesses. When you try something new, pay attention to the aspects of the activity that come naturally to you, as well as the areas where you may struggle.

To help you, here is a limited list of Strengths. Feel free to add strengths that you exhibit that are not on the list on the following page.

Strengths:
Below is a list of 30 behavior-based strengths along with their definitions.

A—D

Adaptability
The ability to adjust and thrive in changing circumstances

Analytical Thinking
The capacity to analyze problems and make logical decisions.

Assertiveness
The ability to effectively express thoughts, opinions, and needs.

Attention to Detail
Being meticulous and thorough

Collaboration
Working effectively with others towards common goals.

Communication
Expressing ideas and information clearly and effectively.

Creativity
Generating innovative and unique ideas and solutions.

Critical Thinking
Evaluating information and making appropriate judgments.

E—J

Empathy
Understanding and sharing the feelings of others.

Flexibility
Being open-minded and adaptable to new situations.

Initiative
Taking independent action and going beyond what is expected.

Integrity
Demonstrating honesty, ethical behavior, and moral principles.

K–N

Leadership
Guiding and inspiring others toward a specific goal.

Listening
Actively paying attention and comprehending others' perspectives.

Motivation
Being driven and enthusiastic about achieving goals.

Negotiation
Finding mutually beneficial outcomes in conflicts or discussions.

O–Q

Organization
Planning, prioritizing, and managing tasks effectively.

Patience
Remaining calm and tolerant in challenging situations.

Perseverance
Persisting and staying committed in the face of obstacles.

Problem Solving
Identifying, analyzing, and resolving complex issues.

R–S

Reliability
Being dependable and trustworthy in fulfilling obligations.

Resilience
Bouncing back from setbacks and maintaining a positive attitude.

Self-Discipline
The ability to control one's actions and impulses for optimal effects.

Self-Motivation
Internal drive and enthusiasm for tasks.

T–Z

Teamwork
Collaborating and cooperating effectively within a group.

Time Management
Allocating time wisely and efficiently.

Tolerance
Accepting and respecting diverse opinions and beliefs.

Trustworthiness
Being honest, reliable, and worthy of confidence.

Versatility
Adapting and performing well in various roles and situations.

Remember that strengths can vary from person to person, and it's essential to identify and nurture your unique strengths to maximize your potential.

My Top 3 Strengths:

....

....

....

....

To help you here is a limited list of Weaknesses. Feel free to add weaknesses that you exhibit that are not on the list below.

Weaknesses

Below is a list of 30 behavior-based weaknesses along with their definitions.

Being easily distracted
Having difficulty staying focused on tasks or priorities, often leading to decreased productivity and increased errors.

Being indecisive
Struggling to make timely and confident decisions, resulting in delays, missed opportunities, and a lack of progress.

Being overly critical of oneself and others
Engaging in constant self-criticism or excessively criticizing others, which can harm self-esteem and strain relationships.

Being overly defensive
Reacting defensively or becoming easily offended when receiving feedback or facing criticism, hindering personal growth and effective communication.

Being too risk-averse
Avoiding or resisting taking reasonable risks, which can limit personal growth and impede progress.

Difficulty in adapting to change
Resistance or discomfort when faced with new situations or unexpected changes, hindering the ability to adjust and thrive.

Difficulty in accepting feedback
Resistance or defensiveness when receiving constructive criticism or suggestions for improvement.

Difficulty accepting responsibility
Avoiding or deflecting accountability for one's actions, often resulting in strained relationships and a lack of personal growth.

Difficulty setting boundaries
Struggling to establish and maintain clear boundaries in personal or professional relationships, leading to exploitation, stress, or burnout.

Disorganized work environment
Having a cluttered or chaotic workspace, which can impede productivity and make it difficult to find necessary resources or information.

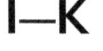
I–K

Impulsiveness
Acting without thinking through the consequences, often leading to hasty decisions or reckless behavior.

Inability to delegate tasks effectively
Reluctance or inability to assign appropriate tasks to others, resulting in an overwhelming workload and limited ability to focus on higher-level responsibilities.

Inability to handle stress and pressure
Difficulty in managing and coping with high-pressure situations, resulting in decreased performance, anxiety, or burnout.

Inability to prioritize tasks effectively
Struggling to identify and focus on the most important tasks or goals, resulting in poor time management and inefficient use of resources.

Inconsistent work habits
Lack of regularity or reliability in completing tasks, meeting deadlines, or maintaining a consistent level of effort.

Ineffective communication skills
Challenges in expressing thoughts, ideas, or instructions clearly and concisely, leading to misunderstandings or ineffective collaboration.

Inflexibility
Resistance or reluctance to adapt to changing circumstances or alternative approaches, hindering progress and innovation.

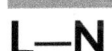

Lack of assertiveness
Difficulty in expressing one's needs, opinions, or boundaries effectively, often resulting in being taken advantage of or not having one's voice heard.

Lack of attention to detail
Overlooking or neglecting important details, leading to errors, oversight, or subpar work quality.

Lack of empathy
Inability to understand or relate to the feelings, perspectives, and experiences of others, resulting in poor interpersonal relationships.

Lack of organization
Having a disorganized work style, resulting in difficulty in finding information, meeting deadlines, or managing tasks efficiently.

Lack of self-confidence
Low belief in one's own abilities, skills, or worth, which can hinder personal growth and limit achievement.

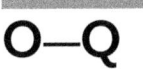

Over-promising and under-delivering
Making commitments or setting expectations that cannot be met, leading to disappointment, damaged trust, and decreased credibility.

Overly emotional reactions
Reacting excessively or disproportionately to situations or events, making it challenging to maintain composure or make rational decisions.

Perfectionism
Setting excessively high standards for oneself and/or others, often leading to dissatisfaction, self-doubt, and impaired productivity.

Poor conflict resolution skills
Inability to handle conflicts or disagreements constructively, often leading to unresolved issues or strained relationships.

Poor time management
Inability to allocate time efficiently, leading to missed deadlines or rushing to complete tasks.

Procrastination
Delaying or postponing tasks unnecessarily, leading to decreased productivity.

R–Z

Resistance to collaboration and teamwork
Reluctance or difficulty in working effectively with others, resulting in strained relationships and suboptimal outcomes.

Tendency to micromanage
Excessive need for control and involvement in every detail of a task or project, often demoralizing team members and impeding their productivity.

Remember that these weaknesses can be improved through self-awareness, intentional effort, and targeted development strategies.

My Top 3 Weaknesses:

....

....

....

....

Now it is time to create a T-Chart with your strengths and weaknesses data that you collected.

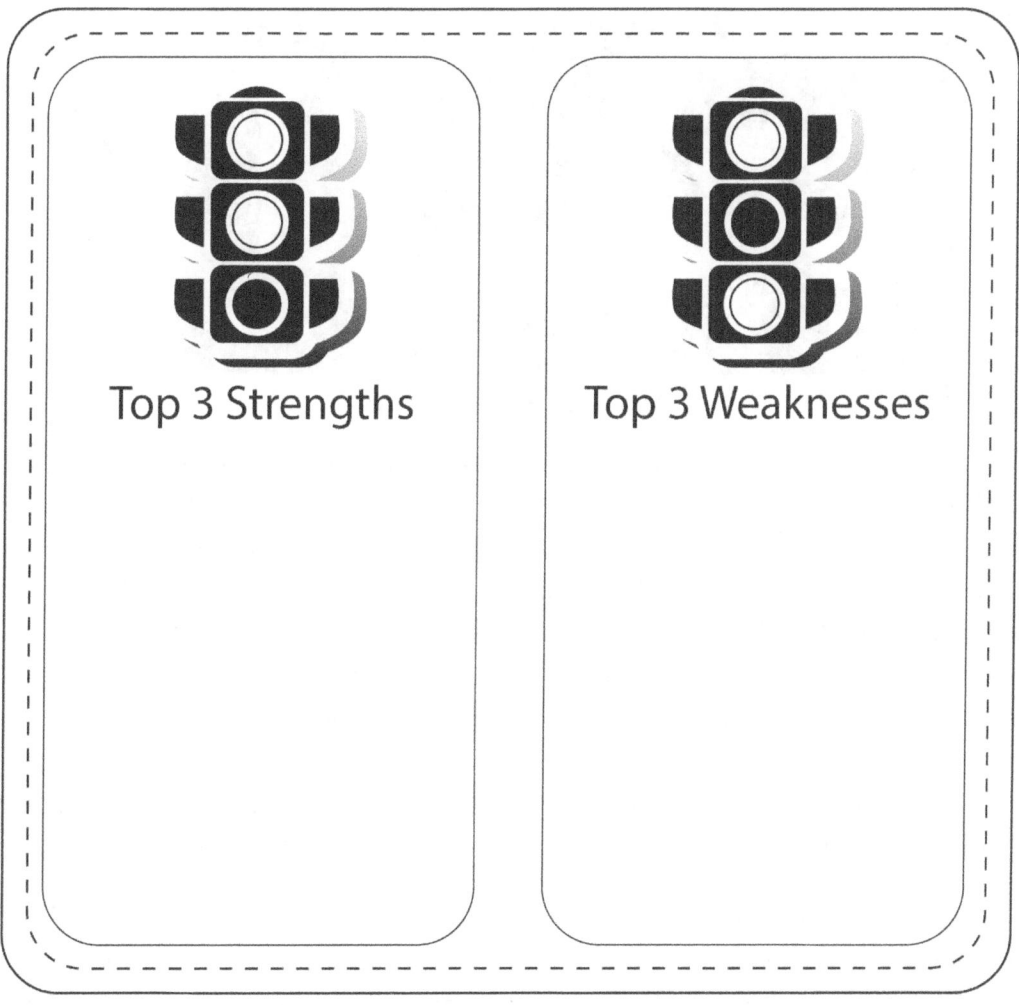

Through the work that I have done for over 25 years with my clients I have found that most often overusing your strengths can become your weakness. As you observe your T-Chart above what observations can you make. You can also look at your strengths and weaknesses from the lens of what are your super powers and what is your kryptonite?

Once you have identified your ID you will notice that it is both your superpower and your kryptonite. Here is an example:

SUPERPOWER: When the ID "to please" is harnessed effectively, it can enable individuals to excel in their relationships, careers, and personal lives. They have a strong desire to satisfy and meet the needs of others, which can lead to high levels of empathy, consideration, and responsiveness. This superpower can make them highly attuned to the emotions and desires of those around them, allowing them to build deep connections and foster a positive environment. Their ability to please others can be a source of joy and fulfillment, as they find satisfaction in bringing happiness to those they care about. This superpower can also manifest as a strong work ethic and a drive for excellence, as they strive to meet and exceed expectations.

KRYPTONITE: However, the ID "to please" can also become a kryptonite when taken to the extreme or when individuals neglect their own needs and well-being in the process. Constantly seeking validation and approval from others can lead to a loss of personal identity and a diminished sense of self-worth. The fear of disappointing others or facing conflict can drive individuals to avoid asserting their own opinions, needs, and boundaries, causing them to become overwhelmed, stressed, or burnt out. Their desire to please can make them vulnerable to manipulation and exploitation by others who may take advantage of their accommodating nature. Ultimately, this ID can become a source of self-neglect, as they prioritize the happiness of others over their own, leading to a sense of emptiness and dissatisfaction.

The ID "to please" can be a superpower when balanced with self-care and healthy boundaries, enabling individuals to form strong connections and excel in various aspects of life. However, it can turn into a kryptonite when taken to extremes, resulting in a loss of personal identity and neglect of one's own needs and well-being.

If someone had an ID "to please" their strengths and weaknesses might look like this:

Strengths:

Empathy: Individuals driven to please tend to possess a high level of empathy. They are able to deeply understand and relate to the emotions and needs of others, making them compassionate and supportive companions.

Adaptability: People with an ID to please often have a remarkable ability to adapt to different situations and accommodate the preferences of those around them. They can easily adjust their behavior and approach to meet the expectations and desires of others.

Relationship Building: Individuals with a strong desire to please excel at building and nurturing relationships. They invest time and effort in understanding others, fostering strong connections, and creating a harmonious environment, which can lead to meaningful and long-lasting relationships.

Weaknesses:

Over commitment: The ID to please can lead individuals to take on too many responsibilities or tasks, often stretching themselves thin. They may struggle to say no or set boundaries, resulting in excessive commitments and a lack of time and energy for their own needs.

Self-neglect: People driven to please often prioritize the happiness and well-being of others over their own. They may neglect self-care, ignore their own needs, and struggle with setting aside time for personal growth and fulfillment.

Conflict Avoidance: The fear of disappointing or upsetting others can cause individuals with the ID to please to avoid conflict at all costs. They may find it challenging to express their true opinions or stand up for themselves, leading to suppressed emotions and potential resentment over time.

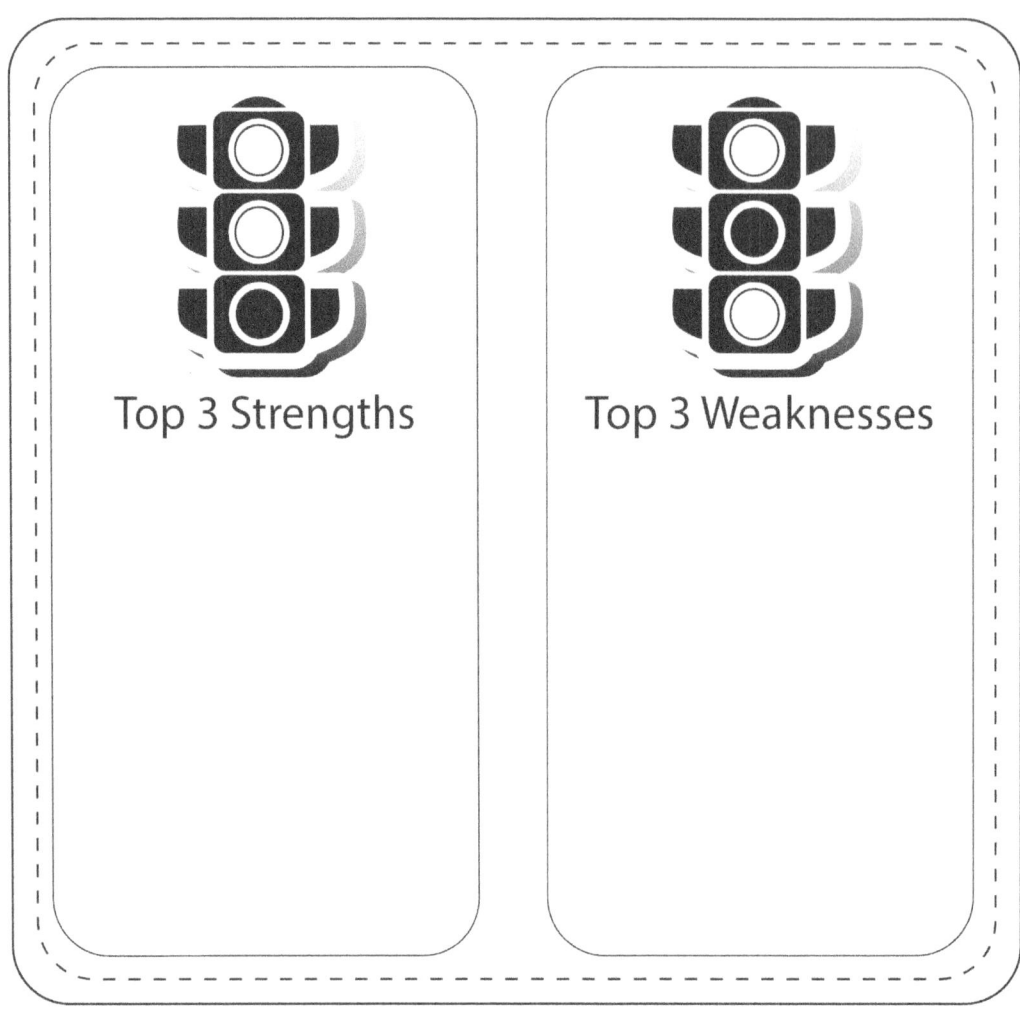

Rewrite your top three strengths and weaknesses again on the above T-Chart. What observations are you making? Is there a connection between your strengths and weaknesses?

Once you have identified your strengths and weaknesses, it's important to reflect on how they relate to your ID. Your ID is the underlying reason why you do what you do—it's the thing that drives you to pursue your goals and ambitions.

What three ID phrases are starting to show up as a reoccurring theme?

You are slowly beginning to collect data from your Present Experiences to weave together with your Past Experiences to find the common thread: your ID.

Energy and Passion

Let's now explore your Energy and Passion, what is your EP equation that will help you shed light on your ID? Your Energy + Passion = Flow State.

The Synergy of Energy and Passion: Unlocking the Flow State

In the pursuit of success and fulfillment, many individuals strive to find that magical state of heightened focus, creativity, and productivity known as the flow state. This elusive state of mind, popularized by psychologist Mihaly Csikszentmihalyi, is characterized by a seamless blend of total immersion, optimal performance, and deep enjoyment. While achieving flow may seem challenging, harnessing the power of energy and passion can pave the way to unlocking this remarkable state. Let's explore how energy and passion synergize to facilitate the flow state, enabling you to tap into your full potential and reach new heights of achievement.

Understanding the Flow State: Before delving into the role of energy and passion, it is crucial to comprehend the nature of the flow state. Csikszentmihalyi describes it as a mental state in which individuals are fully absorbed in an activity, feeling energized, focused, and even losing track of time. Flow occurs when the challenge level of a task matches one's skill level, creating a state of "optimal experience".

Look at the questions below and please respond:

When do you lose track of time and become completely immersed in an activity?

_____

_____

_____

_____

_____

What activities bring you a sense of effortless focus and deep concentration?

_____

_____

_____

_____

_____

What tasks or hobbies make you feel a natural sense of joy and fulfillment?

_____

_____

_____

_____

_____

Are there any specific activities where you feel like your skills perfectly match the challenges you face?

Do you experience a sense of heightened awareness and a feeling of being "in the zone" while engaged in certain activities? If so, what are those activities?

Energy as a Catalyst: Energy, both physical and mental, serves as a fundamental catalyst for achieving and sustaining the flow state. When your body and mind are energized, you are more alert, attentive, and responsive. Several key factors contribute to the energetic component of flow:

Physical Vitality: Engaging in regular physical exercise, maintaining a healthy lifestyle, and ensuring adequate rest and recovery can significantly impact your energy levels. Regular exercise releases endorphins, enhances cognitive function, and promotes overall well-being, creating a solid foundation for the flow state.

How does physical activity impact your energy levels throughout the day?

Provide examples of specific exercises or activities that boost physical vitality and increase overall energy?

_____
_____
_____
_____
_____

What role does nutrition play in maintaining high energy levels and supporting physical vitality?

_____
_____
_____
_____
_____

Are there any lifestyle factors or habits that can negatively affect both physical vitality and energy levels?

_____
_____
_____
_____
_____

Emotional Well-being: Emotional energy, including enthusiasm, positivity, and a sense of purpose, fuels the flow state. Cultivating a growth mindset, practicing gratitude, and managing stress effectively contribute to emotional well-being, enabling you to tap into your potential with greater ease.

How does your emotional well-being impact your energy level throughout the day? Are there specific emotions that tend to drain your energy or uplift it?

Are there any patterns or connections between your emotional state and your energy levels? For example, do you find that when you're feeling stressed or anxious, your energy tends to be lower?

Are there any activities or practices that you engage in to improve your emotional well-being, and have you noticed any corresponding changes in your energy levels as a result?

How do you think taking care of your emotional well-being can positively influence your overall energy levels and productivity? Can you think of any specific examples from your own experiences?

....

....

....

Passion: The Fire Within: Passion, often described as an intense desire or love for an activity or pursuit, serves as a driving force that propels individuals towards the flow state. Here's how passion plays a pivotal role:

Intrinsic Motivation: Passion naturally brings forth intrinsic motivation, which is essential for engaging in activities that lead to flow. When you genuinely enjoy what you do, you are more likely to be intrinsically motivated, leading to increased effort, perseverance, and immersion in your chosen endeavors.

What activities or tasks do you find yourself naturally drawn to and enjoy doing, regardless of external rewards or recognition?

....

....

....

What goals or aspirations have you set for yourself that excite and inspire you on a personal level, even if they require significant effort and time to achieve?

....

....

....

When faced with challenges or setbacks, do you feel a strong inner determination to overcome them and persist in pursuing your goals?

Reflecting on your past experiences, have you ever lost track of time or become completely absorbed in an activity because you were so deeply engaged and interested in it?

Focus and Concentration: Passion directs your attention and allows you to concentrate fully on the task at hand. When you are deeply passionate about something, distractions fade away, and you become fully absorbed in the present moment, leading to heightened focus and facilitating the flow state.

How does focus and concentration contribute to discovering your passion and purpose in life?

Recall a time when you were deeply focused and engaged in a task or activity? How did that experience make you feel, and did it align with your personal interests or values?

....

....

....

....

....

Have you ever noticed that when you are fully concentrating on a particular task, time seems to fly by, and you feel a sense of fulfillment? What do these experiences suggest about your potential passions?

....

....

....

....

Reflect on moments when you have effortlessly maintained your concentration and felt a strong sense of motivation. What were the underlying factors or qualities of those activities that resonated with your inner drive or sense of purpose?

....

....

....

....

....

The Synergy of Energy and Passion

Energy and passion are interconnected and mutually reinforcing elements that amplify the likelihood of entering the flow state:

Energy fuels passion. High energy levels fuel your passion by providing the necessary drive and enthusiasm to pursue your goals relentlessly. With abundant energy, you can overcome obstacles, push through challenges, and maintain sustained effort, enhancing your chances of experiencing flow.

Passion enhances energy. Passion ignites a fire within us, generating intrinsic motivation and resilience. This passion acts as a renewable energy source, enabling you to tap into your inner reservoirs and sustain your efforts over extended periods, even when faced with setbacks.

The flow state is a pinnacle of human experience that combines optimal performance, fulfillment, and enjoyment. By understanding the vital role that energy and passion play in achieving flow, you can cultivate your physical and emotional vitality while pursuing your passions wholeheartedly. The synergy of energy and passion provides the foundation for unlocking the flow state, allowing you to reach your full potential and experience extraordinary levels of productivity, creativity, and fulfillment in your chosen endeavors.

By examining the intersection of your passion, energy, and flow state, you can gain valuable insights into your individual ID—the core motivation that propels you forward and gives meaning to your pursuits. When you engage in activities that align with your passion, energize you, and induce a flow state, you are likely operating in harmony with your ID. This alignment leads to a greater sense of purpose, fulfillment, and personal growth. Understanding your ID can guide your decision-making, goal-setting, and overall direction in life, ultimately enabling you to live a more authentic and purpose-driven existence.

List your biggest takeaways from reading about energy and passion below:

What connections do you see with your strengths and weaknesses?

What connections do you see with your Past Experiences?

What might be 1 to 3 IDs that are surfacing for you?

Present Experiences: Feedback from Others

Seeking feedback from others can be a powerful tool in identifying your ID, the underlying motivation that fuels your actions and ambitions. Often, you are so close to your own thoughts and feelings that it becomes difficult to gain a clear perspective on your true motivations. By seeking feedback from trusted individuals, such as mentors, friends, or colleagues, you can gain valuable insights into your behaviors, patterns, and underlying motivations that may not be apparent to you.

External feedback provides an objective viewpoint that can challenge your assumptions and help you see yourself from a different angle. Others may observe patterns in your actions or behaviors that you may not have noticed or acknowledged. They can highlight strengths, weaknesses, and areas for improvement that may align or contradict with your self-perception. Through open and honest conversations, feedback can reveal patterns of behavior that consistently drive you, illuminate your passions and interests, and uncover the values and principles that guide your decision-making.

Feedback allows you to broaden your perspectives and consider alternative viewpoints. It helps you challenge your biases and preconceived notions, enabling you to see beyond your own limitations. By seeking feedback, you expose yourself to diverse perspectives and experiences, opening yourself up to new ideas and possibilities. This process can expand your understanding of yourself and your motivations, leading to personal growth and a clearer understanding of what truly drives you internally.

Seeking feedback from others can be instrumental in identifying your ID. It provides an external perspective that can help you recognize patterns, strengths, weaknesses, and values that may be hidden or unconscious to you. By inviting feedback and considering alternative viewpoints, you can gain a deeper understanding of yourself, your motivations, and the driving forces behind your actions and aspirations. Below are some questions to consider asking others for feedback.

What am I known for?

....

....

....

What behaviors and actions do I exhibit habitually?

What is my brand?

After gaining clarity regarding the above questions by asking for feedback, what did you learn about yourself?

Do you see patterns that are leading you closer to identifying your ID?

ABC's for Success: Awareness, Behaviors, Connections

Congratulations, that was a lot of hard work and effort on your part. Sometimes examining the past and the present can be both challenging and exciting. You did the heavy lifting and the hard work required to ultimately identify your ID.

Now, you will tie this all together to help you along your journey.

Let's pull all the information that you have collected so far and put it into one succinct place. Below, add information you have gathered about yourself from all of these areas.

Past Experiences

People and Places who have shaped your story?

Values and Beliefs that were shared and instilled into your story?

Present Experiences

Strengths and Weaknesses?

Energy and Passion?

Feedback from Others?

How to Embrace Your 'ID'

You have now discovered your 'ID' and realize that it is the driving force behind your actions, decisions, and goals. It is the thing that gives you a sense of purpose and fulfillment in life. Embracing your 'ID' means acknowledging its importance in your life and making choices that align with it. Here are some steps to help you embrace your 'ID':

Write your 'ID' below:

....

Understand your ID's value: Once you have identified your 'ID', take some time to reflect on why it is important to you. Consider how your ID has influenced your choices and actions in the past. Write your responses below.

....

....

....

....

Live in alignment with your ID: Embracing your 'ID' means making choices that align with it. This may mean setting goals that reflect your motivator, seeking out experiences that fulfill it, and avoiding activities that do not. What do you need to focus on to live in alignment with your ID?

....

....

....

....

Embrace growth and change: Embracing your 'ID' may require you to make changes in your life. Be open to new experiences and growth opportunities that will help you live in alignment with your motivator.

What changes do you need to make to embrace growth and change?

> **TIP**
>
> Remember, embracing your 'ID' is a journey, not a destination. It takes time and effort to fully understand and live in alignment with your purpose, but the benefits are well worth it.

The Benefits of Living in Alignment with Your Motivator

Living in alignment with your 'ID' can have a powerful impact on your life. Here are just a few of the benefits:

Increased happiness and fulfillment: When you are living in alignment with your 'ID', you are more likely to feel a sense of purpose and fulfillment in your life. This can lead to greater happiness and overall life satisfaction.

Improved decision-making: When you are clear on your 'ID', you are better able to make decisions that align with it. This can help you avoid making choices that do not serve your purpose or bring you closer to your goals.

Greater motivation and drive: When you are living in alignment with your 'ID', you are more likely to feel motivated and driven to pursue your goals. This can help you overcome obstacles and achieve success.

Improved relationships: When you are living in alignment with your 'ID', you are more likely to attract people who share your values and goals. This can lead to stronger, more fulfilling relationships.

Greater sense of self-awareness: Embracing your 'ID' requires a deep understanding of yourself and your values. This can help you develop a greater sense of self-awareness and a stronger sense of identity.

Now that you have identified your ID, you will take a deeper look at how it plays out in your life.

Examine Past & Present

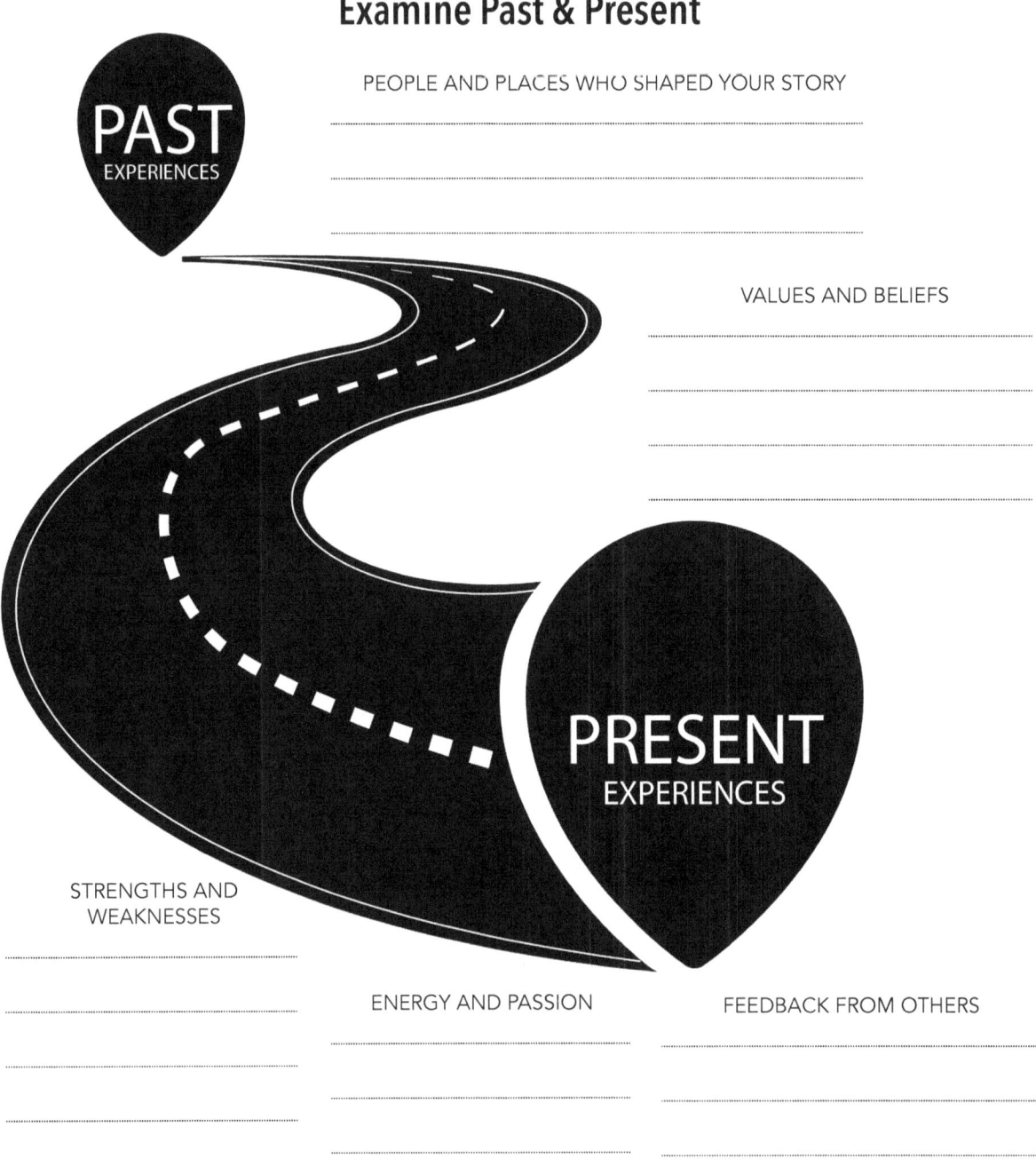

PAST EXPERIENCES

PEOPLE AND PLACES WHO SHAPED YOUR STORY

VALUES AND BELIEFS

PRESENT EXPERIENCES

STRENGTHS AND WEAKNESSES

ENERGY AND PASSION

FEEDBACK FROM OTHERS

"Behavior is the mirror in which everyone shows their image."

–Johann Wolfgang von Goethe

CORE-BEHAVIORS

CONGRATULATIONS YOU ARE now one step closer to Self-Awareness. You have put in the hard work of self-reflection and have discovered your ID. By knowing this data point about yourself, you have gained great wisdom and insight into why you do what you do.

On this journey, in Part 2 of this book – EVIDENCE, you are discovering what we call Core-Behaviors.

Core-behavior is your ability to identify your ID and to consciously reflect as an observer when your ID is not serving you or anyone else around you. You will take a deep dive examination into your behaviors to adjust and modify based on circumstances or situations.

By consciously naming your ID, you are better able to understand your tendencies across situations. A solid understanding of your tendencies helps you make sense of your behaviors. *Behaviors are natural occurrences that result from an emotional response.*

Most often you have your own private motivators for what you do. When things are working well, and situations are driven by your ID, this leads to being content. When situations, circumstance, and people don't align to your ID, events can quickly take a different turn. Differences of thought and opinion can lead to heated, emotionally driven conversations which results in strained relationships.

Just as you are curious about your ID, we invite you to become curious of other's IDs.

Neuroscience tells you that you are not a slave to your emotions. With the right approach, you can choose how you handle situations. You can even choose how emotional you are, and where your emotions take you. Changes in your brain truly can be self-directed.

Not so many years ago talking about emotions was taboo, especially in the workplace. Today, courses in teaching, developing, and exhibiting emotional intelligence are commonplace, thanks to the groundbreaking work of Daniel Goleman.

Before you begin with some exercises, you need to address "what is the importance of core-behaviors?" This book is a guided discovery self-exploration book. Your job is to interact along the way to make this YOUR story. So, let's start with the first question:

What is the importance of knowing your ID?

....
....
....
....
....

How does knowing your ID help you with becoming aware of your behaviors? How does this help with overall Emotional Intelligence?

....
....
....
....
....

Awareness is the foundation that will help you navigate through so many basic life situations. The effort that you are putting into this work will have a wide range of applications creating positive life experiences.

By knowing your ID, you will create better understanding into what drives you in the following core areas:

1. Communication
2. Decision Making
3. Listening
4. Accountability
5. Stress Tolerance
6. Empathy
7. Change Tolerance
8. Flexibility
9. Trust and so much more.

Pick one of the core areas listed above and describe how your ID interacts with it?

_____

_____

_____

_____

_____

Are you beginning to gain further insight into your Core-Awareness? Our hope is that the following self-reflection tools will help with that discovery.

YOUR ID CAN INFLUENCE YOUR BEHAVIORS AND ACTIONS.

For example, someone whose ID is achievement may exhibit behaviors such as setting high goals, working hard to achieve them, and seeking recognition for their accomplishments. On the other hand, someone whose ID is connection may exhibit behaviors such as building strong relationships, seeking to understand others, and prioritizing social interactions.

Understanding your ID can help you align your behaviors and actions with your values and goals. By identifying your ID and the resulting behaviors, you can make conscious choices that support your personal growth and fulfillment.

To help solidify the connection between your ID and your behaviors, think of a recent situation where you made a decision or took an action that aligned, you're your ID.

Write the situation below and describe how your ID influenced your behavior.

....

....

....

....

How did the outcome of the situation align with your 'ID'?

....

....

....

....

Reflection

How does your 'ID' impact your daily life and decision-making?

....

....

....

....

Are there any behaviors or actions that you have exhibited in the past that may have been influenced by your ID? If so, what were they and how did they impact the situation?

How can you use this understanding of your 'ID' to make better decisions and take actions that align with your values and goals?

Is there anything you can do to refine the balance of your ID?

Now, you will explore the following tools to better understand your ID and the behaviors of your ID.

The activities below are suggestions for you to complete. You can complete all of them or you can pick a couple to complete. Remember this is your journey and everyone's journey is unique.

The purpose of these activities is to help you collect EVIDENCE. While examining, you will create a better understanding of yourself while increasing your Core-behaviors. As you complete each activity think about how your *ID* impacts each area.

> **Core-Behaviors Activities**
>
> 1. Boundary Setting
> 2. Feel Your Emotions
> 3. Journal Your Emotions
> 4. Observe Yourself
> 5. Lights On, Lights Off
> 6. Stop doing, Do less of, Keep doing, Do more of, Start doing
> 7. Fear and your ID
> 8. Internal and External Motivation
> 9. Habits
> 10. When I am at my best
> 11. When I am at my worst
> 12. Superpower vs. Kryptonite

1. Boundary Setting

You might be thinking what is boundary setting? How does that relate to ID' and Core Awareness?

Simply speaking, boundaries are the foundation of every relationship you have, including yourself.

The definition that we will use for boundaries is ,"The limits you set around what feels appropriate in your life."

Since you have been focusing on YOU, this activity will help you identify areas that you might not be aware of.

You need to lead yourself first before you can effectively lead others.

You might have heard the term "self-care" in recent years. An important part of self-care is creating and understanding your boundaries. Healthy boundary setting can create an understanding of what you have responsibility for, what is outside of your control, and that tricky area in between.

The healthier your boundaries are, the greater your capacity to offer empathy to others. You are responsible for what happens inside you and for the ways you act and relate to others. You will explore this more when you get to the chapter Core-Connections.

If you have never set a boundary before you are not alone. Depending on what your ID' is, the harder it might be for you to set a boundary. This activity will help you with setting needed boundaries that help you use your ID as your super power and not as your kryptonite.

We have been taught that it's not okay to meet our own needs, have our own space, or protect/project our own energy. As you practice setting boundaries you will become more comfortable and begin to wonder how you ever lived without them.

How Healthy Are My Boundaries?

If you agree with a statement, below put a check next to it. Then one-by-one reflect on and consider why you checked it. Does it connect to your ID? Is it giving you greater Core-Awareness?

- ☐ *I do too much*
- ☐ *I do things out of obligation*
- ☐ *Many people rely on me*
- ☐ *I neglect my needs*
- ☐ *I give constantly*
- ☐ *I am focused on helping others*
- ☐ *I feel anxious or panicked when other people are not okay*
- ☐ *I was taught to put others before myself*
- ☐ *I feel responsible for other people's emotions*
- ☐ *I feel so drained by all my responsibilities*

- ☐ *I take on the emotions of others around me*
- ☐ *I feel destabilized if someone doesn't like me*
- ☐ *I am sensitive to criticism*
- ☐ *I feel guilty easily*
- ☐ *I find myself doing things I don't want to do*
- ☐ *I don't speak up when I am treated poorly*
- ☐ *I feel unable to say no*
- ☐ *I feel unable to make decisions*
- ☐ *I can't relax*
- ☐ *I expect other people to anticipate my needs*

- ☐ *I discount my own thoughts, opinions, and intuition*
- ☐ *I don't invest many resources into my own dreams*
- ☐ *I am uncomfortable being served or pampered*
- ☐ *I grew up with adults with poor boundaries*
- ☐ *I contain anger until it suddenly explodes*
- ☐ *I don't let people get to close to me*

Some Reminders

! Boundaries are kind. By giving others clear communication around how you want to be treated is a form of self-love. It also shows respect to the other person that you care about them enough to communicate your needs.

! You cannot control how other people respond to your boundaries. What you can control is how you defend those boundaries even if you are not comfortable.

! Be proactive and responding instead of reacting.

! Practice setting your boundaries and don't feel the need to over-explain or apologize for them.

! Accept the other person's response without acting to change it.

SIMPLE BOUNDARIES SOUND LIKE

- "Right now, isn't good for me."
- "I'll need some time to think about that; I'll get back to you."
- "That's just not going to work for me."
- "I'm not available."
- "Thank you for the invite, that is something I can't do right now."
- "I don't feel comfortable talking about this."
- "No."

QUESTIONS FOR REFLECTION

In what situations would it be important to create boundaries?

....

....

....

....

What are your boundaries trying to protect?

What is important to you?

How does your ID impact the way you set boundaries or don't set boundaries?

What have you learned that gives you more Core-Awareness?

Feel Your Emotions
EMOTIONALLY INTELLIGENT CHANGE

I feel (emotion) _____
because _____
and I will (action) _____
so that _____

Insight:

2. FEEL YOUR EMOTIONS

Core-Awareness is your ability to understand and accurately perceive your emotions in the moment and to realize your tendencies during all situations. This takes time and by doing the hard work and activities in this book it will help you with your journey.

One of the activities that will help you stay on top of your typical go to behavior (reactions) is "Feeling Your Emotion". A keen understanding of your behavior, reactions, and tendencies quickly aids in making sense of your emotions.

How many times do you hit the pause button during the day to acknowledge your emotions? And how often do you check in with your emotions to see if they are working for you or against you while developing your Core-Awareness?

This activity will allow you to stop and be willing to experience the discomfort of focusing on a feeling that may be negative or uncomfortable. This information can help you better understand your emotions and what positive action you can take.

3. JOURNALING YOUR EMOTIONS

Journaling your emotions is a powerful activity that can help you gain insight into your inner world, improve your emotional intelligence, and reduce stress and anxiety. The practice involves setting aside time each day to write down your thoughts and feelings, without judgment or censorship.

When you journal your emotions, you create a safe space to explore your thoughts and feelings in a non-threatening way. You can express your emotions openly and honestly without worrying about how others may perceive you. This can help you gain a deeper understanding of your emotions, as well as the triggers and patterns that contribute to them.

In addition to helping you understand and process your emotions, journaling can also help you regulate them. By writing down your thoughts and feelings, you can gain perspective and distance yourself from them. This can help you view your emotions more objectively and respond to them in a more constructive way. Over time, regular journaling can help you develop greater emotional awareness, resilience, and self-compassion.

When your ID is threatened you become charged in the moment. By journaling your emotions you can find the cause of your emotions for example:

- I felt unheard
- I felt judged
- I felt disrespected
- I didn't feel good enough
- I felt unimportant
- I felt controlled
- I didn't feel worthy
- I felt left out
- I felt uncared for
- I felt unloved
- I felt blamed
- I felt betrayed

By answering and reflecting on the seven questions below you will begin to gain clarity over your behaviors and be able to choose appropriate actions next time you are in a similar situation.

What happened?

....
....
....
....

Your feelings you experienced around the situation?

....
....
....
....
....

People involved?

....
....
....

ABC's for Success: Awareness, Behaviors, Connections

The moment you felt 'charged'?

The results?

How do you think it should have been solved?

What makes it hard to let go?

4. Observe Yourself

Observing yourself is a powerful tool for self-awareness, personal growth, and self-improvement. By paying attention to your thoughts, emotions, and behaviors in different situations, you can gain insights into your strengths, weaknesses, and patterns of behavior. This can help you identify areas where you want to change, learn new skills, or develop new habits to achieve your goals.

To begin observing yourself, start by setting aside time each day to reflect on your experiences. This could be through journaling, meditation, or simply taking a few minutes to think about your day. Ask yourself questions like: What did I do well today? What challenges did I face? How did I respond to those challenges? What emotions did I experience, and how did they affect my behavior?

As you become more comfortable with observing yourself, try to expand your focus to include different aspects of your life. For example, you might observe your communication style with different people, your eating habits, or your time management skills. By observing yourself in different situations, you can gain a more comprehensive understanding of your behavior and identify areas where you want to make changes.

TIP

Remember, observing yourself is not about judging yourself or being critical. It is about becoming more aware of your thoughts, emotions, and behaviors so that you can make conscious choices that align with your values and goals. With practice, you can develop a deeper level of self-awareness and use this knowledge to create the life you want.

What are your observations?

....

....

....

....

What data did you collect about yourself?

_____
_____
_____
_____
_____
_____

What are the connections between what you observed and your ID?

_____
_____
_____
_____
_____
_____
_____
_____

5. LIGHTS ON, LIGHTS OFF

In a general sense, "lights on" and "lights off" are often used as metaphors to describe different behaviors or states of being. Let's explore what these phrases typically represent.

Lights On Behaviors:

Engagement: Being actively present, attentive, and involved in a situation or conversation.

Positivity: Demonstrating a positive attitude, optimism, and a willingness to find solutions or opportunities.

Proactivity: Taking initiative, being self-motivated, and showing a proactive approach to tasks or challenges.

Open-mindedness: Being receptive to new ideas, different perspectives, and feedback from others.

Collaboration: Working well with others, cooperating, and fostering a sense of teamwork.

Empathy: Showing understanding, compassion, and consideration towards others' feelings and needs.

Adaptability: Being flexible and able to adjust to changing circumstances or new information.

Accountability: Taking responsibility for one's actions, owning up to mistakes, and working towards improvement.

Respect: Treating others with respect, valuing their opinions, and maintaining a courteous demeanor.

Growth mindset: Having a mindset that embraces learning, challenges, and continuous personal and professional development.

Lights Off Behaviors:

Disengagement: Being distracted, inattentive, or uninterested in a situation or conversation.

Negativity: Displaying a negative attitude, pessimism, and a focus on problems rather than solutions.

Passivity: Waiting for others to take action or relying heavily on instructions rather than being proactive.

Closed-mindedness: Resisting new ideas, being rigid in one's thinking, and rejecting feedback from others.

Conflict or Competition: Engaging in confrontations, prioritizing personal interests over collaboration, and undermining others.

Lack of empathy: Disregarding or dismissing others' emotions or needs and displaying a self-centered attitude.

Lights Off Behaviors (cont.)

Resistance to change: Being resistant or reluctant to adapt to new circumstances or ideas.

Lack of accountability: Avoiding responsibility, blaming others, or failing to acknowledge one's mistakes.

Disrespect: Behaving rudely, disregarding others' boundaries, and showing a lack of consideration.

Fixed mindset: Having a mindset that avoids challenges, avoids feedback, and believes abilities are static.

It's important to note that these categorizations are generalizations and not everyone will exhibit all behaviors consistently. Additionally, what may be considered "lights on" or "lights off" can vary depending on cultural, social, and personal contexts.

As you reflect on your ID, what 'lights on' behaviors are a byproduct of your ID?

_____

_____

_____

_____

_____

As you reflect on your ID, what 'lights off' behaviors are a byproduct of your ID?

_____

_____

_____

_____

_____

What action do you plan on taking?

....

....

....

....

6. **Stop doing, Do less of, Keep doing, Do more of, Start doing: Personal Behavior Analysis**

The "Stop doing, Do less of, Keep doing, Do more of, Start doing" framework can be a powerful tool for you to reflect on your behaviors and make intentional changes for personal growth and improvement. By assessing current actions and habits, this analysis helps you identify areas for change and focuses your efforts on activities that align with your ID, goals, and values. Here's an overview of each category and its purpose.

STOP DOING: This category involves recognizing behaviors that are no longer serving a positive purpose or hindering personal growth. It encourages you to let go of habits that are unproductive, harmful, or counterproductive. By stopping such behaviors, you can create space for new and more beneficial actions.

DO LESS OF: In this category, the aim is to reduce the frequency or intensity of certain behaviors that may still have some value but could be optimized. It involves identifying activities that consume excessive time, energy, or resources without commensurate benefits. By doing less of such behaviors, you can free up resources for more meaningful pursuits.

KEEP DOING: The keep doing category acknowledges behaviors and habits that contribute to personal well-being, growth, and success. These are actions that align with your ID and have yielded positive outcomes. Recognizing their value helps you maintain these behaviors and leverage them for ongoing personal development.

DO MORE OF: This category emphasizes behaviors or habits that have shown promise or positive outcomes but are not given enough attention or effort. It encourages you to allocate more resources, time, or energy to these activities to further enhance your personal growth and success. Doing more of such behaviors can lead to increased effectiveness and fulfillment.

START DOING: The start doing category prompts you to adopt new behaviors, habits, or strategies that can contribute to personal improvement and success. It involves exploring fresh ideas, acquiring new skills, or pursuing activities that align with personal goals and aspirations. Starting such behaviors opens up possibilities for growth and positive change.

Activity
STEP 1: Self-reflection

Set aside dedicated time for introspection and self-assessment.

Consider various aspects of your life, such as personal goals, relationships, health, and well-being.

Identify behaviors and habits that are relevant to each aspect.

STEP 2: Categorize behaviors

Categorize each behavior or habit into the five categories: Stop doing, Do less of, Keep doing, Do more of, and Start doing.

Be honest and objective in evaluating the impact and alignment of each behavior with your goals and values.

STEP 3: Action plan

Prioritize the behaviors in each category based on their potential impact and importance to you.

Develop a specific action plan for each category, outlining steps and timelines.

Consider seeking support or guidance from mentors, coaches, or trusted individuals who can help you implement changes.

STEP 4: Implementation and evaluation

Start implementing the changes identified in your action plan.

Regularly evaluate your progress, adjusting as needed.

Celebrate milestones and achievements along the way to maintain motivation and momentum.

STEP 5: Continuous improvement

Periodically review and update your behavior analysis, adjusting your action plan as circumstances change.

Embrace a growth mindset and remain open to learning and adapting.

Continuously seek opportunities for personal development and growth.

By engaging in this personal behavior analysis, you can become more self-aware, make intentional choices, and work towards personal growth and success. Regularly revisiting and refining this process allows for ongoing improvement and a more fulfilling life journey.

What was your biggest takeaway from the above activity?

....

....

....

7. Fear and your ID

Fear is a powerful emotion that can significantly impact your ID, which refers to your personal motivation, aspirations, and drive to achieve your goals. When fear takes hold, it can hinder your progress, lead to self-doubt, and limit your potential. However, with awareness and effective strategies, you can overcome fear and regain control of your ID.

Activity

Overcoming Fear and Empowering Your Internal Driver

Identify the fear: Take some time to reflect on the specific fears that are impacting your ID. Is it fear of failure, fear of judgment, or fear of the unknown? Understanding the root causes of your fears will allow you to address them more effectively.

What is your specific fear?

....

....

....

How does your fear relate to your ID?

Challenge limiting beliefs: Fear often stems from limiting beliefs you hold about yourself and your abilities. Identify any negative beliefs that contribute to your fear and question their validity. Ask yourself if there is evidence to support these beliefs or if they are simply assumptions. Replace negative beliefs with positive affirmations that empower and motivate you.

Identify negative beliefs that contribute to your fear:

What evidence do you have to support these beliefs?

What affirmations can you say instead?

Set realistic goals: Break down your larger goals into smaller, manageable tasks. Setting achievable goals not only helps you overcome fear but also builds confidence and momentum. By focusing on one step at a time, you can gradually overcome your fears and make progress towards your larger objectives.

What step will you take today?

Take calculated risks: Fear often arises when you step outside your comfort zone. To overcome it, challenge yourself to take calculated risks. Start with small steps that push your boundaries and gradually increase the level of difficulty. By exposing yourself to new experiences, you will expand your comfort zone and reduce the impact of fear on your ID.

What is your comfort zone and what might it take to step outside of your comfort zone?

Cultivate a growth mindset: Embrace the concept of a growth mindset, which believes that abilities and intelligence can be developed through dedication and hard work. Instead of fearing failure, view it as an opportunity for growth and learning. Emphasize the process rather than the outcome and celebrate your efforts and progress along the way.

What growth mindset do you need to embrace?

_____

_____

_____

_____

Seek support and guidance: Don't hesitate to reach out for support when facing fear. Surround yourself with a positive and encouraging network of family, friends, or mentors who can provide guidance and reassurance. Sharing your fears with others can help alleviate their impact and offer different perspectives.

Who can you reach out to for support?

_____

_____

_____

_____

Practice self-care and self-compassion: Fear can be emotionally draining, so it's crucial to prioritize self-care and self-compassion. Engage in activities that bring you joy and relaxation, such as exercise, mindfulness, hobbies, or spending time in nature. Treat yourself with kindness and understanding, acknowledging that fear is a natural part of growth and that setbacks are opportunities to learn and improve.

What can you do to recharge your batteries?

....

....

....

....

....

> **TIP**
>
> Remember, overcoming fear takes time and effort. Be patient with yourself and celebrate each step forward. By actively addressing your fears and empowering your ID, you can unlock your full potential and achieve your goals with greater confidence and resilience.

8. INTERNAL AND EXTERNAL MOTIVATION

To take a deep dive into your ID and to examine it from an internal and external motivation perspective can help you with your actions and behaviors. Let's look at an example of this.

If someone has an ID to prove their worth, they can be motivated both intrinsically and extrinsically. Let's explore how these motivations might manifest:

INTRINSIC MOTIVATION

Personal Growth and Fulfillment: Individuals may be driven by a deep desire to continually improve themselves, expand their skills, and achieve personal growth. They derive satisfaction and a sense of fulfillment from challenging themselves and reaching new levels of competence or mastery.

Passion and Enjoyment: They may be motivated by a genuine passion for their work or chosen pursuits. The sheer joy and enthusiasm they experience while engaging in activities that align with their interests and strengths become a powerful intrinsic motivator to prove their worth.

Autonomy and Personal Control: Individuals may be motivated by a need for autonomy and the ability to make independent decisions. They derive satisfaction from taking ownership of their actions, being in control of their outcomes, and proving their competence and worth through self-directed efforts.

Extrinsic Motivation

Recognition and Validation: External recognition and validation play a significant role in motivating individuals who seek to prove their worth. They may strive for acknowledgment, praise, and admiration from others, such as superiors, peers, or the broader community. Achieving external validation serves as tangible proof of their capabilities and worth.

Rewards and Incentives: The prospect of external rewards, such as promotions, bonuses, or accolades, can be a strong motivating factor for those driven to prove their worth. They may channel their efforts and talents towards achieving specific targets or goals in anticipation of tangible rewards.

Competition and Comparison: Some individuals are motivated by comparing themselves to others and striving to outperform them. The drive to be better, achieve more, or surpass their peers becomes a significant external motivator to prove their worth by establishing themselves as the best in their field or domain.

It's important to note that intrinsic and extrinsic motivations can coexist and vary in intensity depending on the individual and the context. While intrinsic motivations focus on internal fulfillment and personal satisfaction, extrinsic motivations are driven by external factors and the validation received from others. Understanding and balancing both types of motivation can be instrumental in harnessing one's ID.

Write your ID below:

....

What motivates your ID intrinsically?

....

....

What motivates your ID extrinsically?

9. Habits

Habits play a crucial role in shaping your behavior and determining your outcomes in life. Habits are routines that are repeated regularly, and they can be both positive and negative. Positive habits such as regular exercise, healthy eating, and meditation can improve your physical and mental well-being and help you achieve your goals. On the other hand, negative habits such as smoking, binge eating, or procrastination can harm your health and hinder your progress in life.

Youur behavior is strongly influenced by your habits, and creating new habits or breaking old ones requires a conscious effort. One effective way to create positive habits is to start small, setting achievable goals that can be sustained over time. For instance, if you want to start a regular exercise routine, start with short workouts, and gradually increase the duration and intensity over time. It's also important to celebrate small wins along the way to keep yourself motivated.

Breaking negative habits can be challenging, but it is possible with persistence and determination. Identify the triggers that lead to the negative behavior and find healthy alternatives. For example, if you tend to snack when you're stressed, try replacing unhealthy snacks with fruits or vegetables. Surround yourself with positive influences and seek support from friends or family members who share your goals.

Ultimately, your habits and behaviors shape who you are and the outcomes you achieve in life. By cultivating positive habits and breaking negative ones, you can improve your well-being and achieve your goals.

What habits do I need to be aware of as it relates to my ID?

What habits do I need to let go?

What habits do I need to add?

10. When I Am At My Best

Your ID can lead to unbalance during certain seasons of your life. It can also bring unbalance daily if left unchecked.

Examining "When I Am At My Best" and "When I am At My Worst" helps you identify what you are doing in that particular moment and see if your ID is working for you or if it has run amuck.

Remember, you are the data collector in your story.

Think back to one of your best days in the past week.

What were you doing?

_____
_____
_____
_____

What were you feeling?

_____
_____
_____
_____

What was your energy like?

_____
_____
_____
_____

How does this relate to your ID?

11. When I Am At My Worst

When functioning at your worst, you can tend to feel overwhelmed, stressed, and anxious. Your mind becomes cluttered with negative thoughts, and you might find it difficult to concentrate on anything for an extended period. You may feel irritable and impatient, lashing out at others over small issues. At times, you may withdraw from social interactions and isolate yourself, leading to a sense of loneliness and despair.

When this happens, what is playing out for you?

What is your energy like?

Can you identify how this relates to your ID?

....

....

....

....

12. Superpower vs. Kryptonite

Your behaviors can be both your superpowers and your kryptonite depending on how you utilize them. Here are a few examples:

Perfectionism: Perfectionism can be a superpower when it drives you to strive for excellence and to push yourself to be better. However, it can also be your kryptonite when it leads you to become overly critical of yourself and others, and to obsess over small details that may not matter in the grand scheme of things—or even at all.

Empathy: Empathy can be a superpower when it allows you to connect with others, understand their perspectives, and respond to their needs with kindness and compassion. However, it can also be your kryptonite when you become so absorbed in other people's emotions that you neglect your own well-being or become overwhelmed by the weight of their problems.

Confidence: Confidence can be a superpower when it helps you to take risks, speak up for yourself, and pursue your goals with determination. However, it can also be your kryptonite when it leads you to be overconfident, to underestimate challenges, and to ignore feedback or constructive criticism.

Procrastination: Procrastination can be a superpower when it allows you to work well under pressure, to generate creative solutions, or to prioritize important tasks when time is limited. However, it can also be your kryptonite when it becomes a chronic habit that undermines your productivity, causes you stress and anxiety, and prevents you from reaching your full potential.

Ultimately, it is up to you to recognize your own behavioral patterns and to cultivate core-awareness and self-control so that you can use your behaviors as superpowers and avoid them becoming your kryptonite.

How is your ID your Superpower?

How is your ID your kryptonite?

SUMMARY

Identifying your ID can be a powerful tool for understanding and improving your actions and behaviors. An ID refers to the underlying motivation or core values that guide your decisions and actions. By becoming aware of your ID, you gain insight into what truly matters to you and what fuels your actions.

Understanding your ID helps you align your behaviors with your values. When you are clear about what drives you, you can make choices that are in harmony with your authentic self. This alignment brings a sense of purpose and fulfillment to your actions, as they are driven by your genuine desires rather than external pressures or expectations. For example, if your ID is to be considerate, you may find that your behaviors naturally lean towards acts of kindness and empathy.

Knowing your ID can help you make better decisions. It acts as a compass, guiding you towards choices that are in line with your values and long-term goals. When faced with difficult decisions, you can assess the options based on whether they align with your ID. This clarity provides a sense of direction and prevents you from getting swayed by short-term temptations or societal pressures.

Identifying your ID is a valuable step towards self-awareness and personal growth. It enables you to live a more authentic and purpose-driven life, ensuring that your actions and behaviors are aligned with your values. By tapping into your ID, you can make better choices, find greater fulfillment, and lead a more meaningful existence.

PART THREE: ENGAGEMENT
CORE CONNECTIONS

"I DEFINE CONNECTION AS THE ENERGY THAT EXISTS BETWEEN PEOPLE WHEN THEY FEEL SEEN, HEARD, AND VALUED; WHEN THEY CAN GIVE AND RECEIVE WITHOUT JUDGMENT; AND WHEN THEY DERIVE SUSTENANCE AND STRENGTH FROM THE RELATIONSHIP."

—BRENÉ BROWN

CORE CONNECTIONS

IN THIS PART we will engage with CONNECTIONS. Your ID impacts the way you lead and connect with other individuals. Here we bring meaningful awareness to how you engage with others based off your ID and their ID.

In the realm of human relationships, IDs play a crucial role in shaping your motivations, desires, and actions. When you are aware of your own ID, it allows you to communicate your needs and values more effectively, fostering deeper connections with others. By understanding your own drivers, you can express your desires and intentions clearly, leading to better alignment and understanding within relationships.

However, forging meaningful connections goes beyond self-awareness. It is equally important to discern and comprehend the IDs of others. By actively listening, observing, and engaging in empathetic conversations, you can gain insights into the values, goals, aspirations, and general nature of the people you interact with. Recognizing the drivers that motivate others enables you to build rapport, demonstrate understanding, and respond in ways that resonate with your counterparts. This understanding paves the way for more meaningful and fulfilling connections.

To uncover the IDs of others, you can engage in open-ended conversations, asking questions that elicit personal values, passions, and aspirations. Actively listening to their responses, non-verbal cues, and paying attention to their actions can also provide valuable insights. By showing genuine curiosity, empathy, and a willingness to understand others on a deeper level, you can create an environment that encourages meaningful exchanges and fosters strong connections.

By acknowledging and understanding both your own ID and those of others, you can enhance your ability to connect meaningfully with people. This awareness empowers you to communicate your needs more effectively and respond in ways that resonate with others, cultivating relationships based on understanding, empathy, and shared values.

You will ENGAGE in the following activities/tools to make meaningful connections with others and to identify potential roadblocks, challenges and opportunities.

Core-Connections Activities

1. Be Open and Curious
2. Competing Internal Drivers
3. Listen/Silence
4. DiSC
5. Tackle a Tough Conversation
6. Three Concentric Circles

1. BE OPEN AND CURIOUS

Remaining open and curious about someone else's ID is a valuable skill for building empathy and understanding. Here are some tips to help you cultivate this mindset:

Practice active listening: Give the other person your full attention and listen to what they're saying without interrupting or formulating your response. Show genuine interest in their thoughts and feelings.

Suspend judgment: Avoid making quick assumptions or jumping to conclusions about the other person's beliefs, motives, or intentions. Be aware of your own biases and try to approach the conversation with an open mind.

Ask open-ended questions: Encourage the other person to share more about their perspectives and motivations by asking open-ended questions. This can help you delve deeper into their thoughts and gain a better understanding of their IDs.

Seek to understand, not persuade: Instead of trying to convince the other person of your own viewpoint, focus on understanding theirs. This shift in mindset allows you to explore their ID without the pressure of trying to change their mind.

Empathize with their experiences: Put yourself in the other person's shoes and try to imagine what they might be feeling or experiencing. This empathetic approach can help you connect with their ID on a deeper level.

Be aware of non-verbal cues: Pay attention to the other person's body language, facial expressions, and tone of voice. These non-verbal cues can provide additional insights into their internal state and help you better understand their motivations.

Practice cultural sensitivity: Recognize that people's ID can be influenced by their cultural background, beliefs, and experiences. Be respectful of these differences and avoid making assumptions based on your own cultural lens.

Embrace curiosity: Cultivate a genuine sense of curiosity about others. Approach conversations with the mindset of a learner, eager to discover new perspectives and understand the factors that drive people's actions.

Reflect on your own ID: Understanding your own motivations and biases can help you relate to others more effectively. Reflect on your own ID and how they might influence your perceptions and interactions with others.

Practice patience and tolerance: Recognize that exploring someone else's ID takes time and patience. Be tolerant of different viewpoints and avoid rushing to conclusions. Give the other person the space and time they need to express themselves fully.

By adopting these tips, you can foster a mindset of openness and curiosity, allowing you to better understand and connect with the ID of others.

What above will you implement to gain better understanding of someone's ID?

....
....
....
....

What steps will you take to make sure you are taking everyone's needs into consideration?

....
....
....

How can you check your own ID in relationships?

....

....

....

....

2. Competing Internal Drivers

Interacting with someone who has a competing ID can be challenging but also an opportunity for growth and collaboration. When individuals have different drivers, such as one person being driven to "get it done" and another being driven to "get it right," it's important to find common ground and establish effective communication. Here is an overview and some tips to navigate such a situation.

Recognize and respect differences	Understand that people have diverse motivations and drivers that influence their work style and approach. Acknowledge that both drivers can contribute to success if balanced properly.
Establish open communication	Foster an environment of open dialogue where both parties can express their perspectives and concerns. Encourage active listening and seek to understand each other's viewpoints without judgment.
Find common experiences and goals	Identify shared objectives and goals that align with both drivers. Focus on overarching outcomes that can be achieved by combining the strengths of each approach.
Seek complementary strengths	Recognize the unique strengths each individual brings to the table. Emphasize the importance of both getting things done efficiently and ensuring accuracy. Encourage collaboration and leverage each other's expertise to achieve the best results.

COMMUNICATION TIP	IMPLEMENTATION TIP
Define complementary roles and responsibilities	Clearly define roles and responsibilities based on individual strengths and preferences. Assign tasks that play to each person's driver, allowing them to excel in their areas of expertise.
Compromise and find balance	Strive for a middle ground by finding compromises that satisfy both drivers. Look for solutions that are both efficient and accurate, striking a balance between speed and quality.
Set realistic expectations	Establish clear expectations regarding timelines, deliverables, and quality standards. Ensure that both parties are aware of the agreed-upon parameters, which can help manage potential conflicts arising from differing IDs.
Utilize feedback and constructive criticism	Encourage constructive feedback and criticism from both sides. Recognize that while the "get it done" approach may prioritize speed, the "get it right" approach can provide valuable insights to improve overall quality. Emphasize the importance of learning from each other's perspectives.
Embrace flexibility and adaptability	Be open to adapting your work style and approach to accommodate the differing drivers. Flexibility and willingness to adjust can create a harmonious working relationship and promote a productive environment.
Focus on mutual growth	View the collaboration as an opportunity for personal and professional growth. Encourage each to learn from the other's strengths, expand their skill sets, and develop a more well-rounded approach.

TIP

Remember that working with someone who has a competing ID can lead to better outcomes through the diversity of thought and approaches. By understanding, respecting, and leveraging each other's IDs, you can forge a strong working relationship and achieve success together.

How can this information help you with meaningful connections with others?

What do you need to be aware of?

3. LISTEN/SILENCE

Listening and silence can be powerful tools for developing an understanding of someone else's ID or motivations. Here's how they can help.

Active Listening: Actively listening to someone involves giving them your full attention and focusing on what they are saying, both verbally and non-verbally. By truly listening to their words, tone, and body language, you can gain valuable insights into their thoughts, emotions, and underlying motivations. It allows you to pick up on subtle cues and signals that can provide a deeper understanding of their internal state, plus, of course, the information they are trying to impart.

Empathy and Perspective Taking: Listening attentively to someone's words and experiences helps you develop empathy, the ability to understand and share their feelings. Empathy allows you to put yourself in their shoes and gain a better grasp of their internal drives and motivations. It helps you see the world from their perspective and appreciate their unique experiences, values, and aspirations.

Non-Verbal Cues: Silence can be particularly beneficial when accompanied by non-verbal cues such as nodding, maintaining eye contact, and adopting an open posture. Non-verbal cues can encourage the person to open up and share more about their ID. By remaining silent and attentive, you create a safe and supportive environment that allows them to express themselves freely.

Uncovering Subtext: Sometimes, what remains unsaid is as important as what is spoken. Silence during a conversation can create space for the person to reflect and share deeper thoughts or emotions. They may reveal underlying concerns, fears, or motivations that they might have hesitated to express initially. By allowing such pauses and moments of silence, you give them the opportunity to explore their ID more fully.

Building Trust: Listening attentively and respecting silence can help build trust in your relationship with the person. When they feel heard and understood, they are more likely to open up and share their authentic selves. Trust is a crucial element for gaining insight into someone's ID as they are more likely to be vulnerable and honest when they trust you.

> **TIP**
>
> Remember, everyone is unique, and their IDs can be complex. Listening and silence should be used in conjunction with other forms of communication to develop a holistic understanding of someone's motivations.

What are your thoughts?

....

....

....

....

....

....

What action will you take?

_____
_____
_____
_____

What part of silence and active listening might be challenging for you?

_____
_____
_____
_____

4. DiSC (Dominance, Influence, Steadiness Conscientiousness) / Internal Driver

Knowing someone else's DiSC style and ID can greatly help with creating meaningful connections by providing insights into their communication preferences, motivations, and behavior patterns. Here's how this knowledge can be beneficial:

Improved Communication: DiSC styles (Dominance, Influence, Steadiness, and Conscientiousness) offer valuable information about how individuals prefer to communicate and process information. By understanding someone's DiSC style, you can tailor your communication style to better align with theirs. For example, if someone has a Dominance style, they may appreciate direct and concise communication, while someone with a Steadiness style might prefer a more patient and supportive approach. Adapting your communication to their style fosters better understanding, minimizes misunderstandings, and enhances overall communication effectiveness.

Increased Empathy: Understanding someone's DiSC style and ID can foster empathy and compassion. When you recognize the factors that drive their behavior, it becomes easier to empathize with their perspectives and motivations. By appreciating their unique qualities and inherent strengths, you can develop a deeper understanding of their needs and experiences, leading to more empathetic and meaningful connections.

Enhanced Collaboration: DiSC styles can also provide insights into how individuals prefer to work and collaborate. For instance, someone with an Influence style may thrive in a dynamic and social environment, while a Conscientiousness-oriented person may prefer structure and attention to detail. Recognizing these preferences can help you create a collaborative environment that accommodates everyone's strengths and working styles, leading to improved teamwork and productivity.

Conflict Resolution: DiSC knowledge can be particularly valuable in resolving conflicts and managing differences. By understanding each person's DiSC style, you can identify potential sources of conflict and find ways to bridge gaps. For example, if two individuals with opposing styles have a disagreement, knowing their respective preferences can help you facilitate a constructive conversation by encouraging them to approach the issue in a way that resonates with their styles and IDs.

Building Trust: When you demonstrate an understanding of someone's DiSC style and ID, it signals that you are willing to invest time and effort into knowing and connecting with them on a deeper level. This can build trust and rapport, as individuals appreciate being seen and understood for who they are. Trust is a fundamental element of meaningful connections, and by utilizing the knowledge of DiSC styles, you can foster trust-based relationships.

Understanding someone else's DiSC style and ID can significantly contribute to more meaningful connections by improving communication, fostering empathy, enhancing collaboration, facilitating conflict resolution, and building trust. It provides a framework to appreciate and connect with others in a way that aligns with their preferences and motivations, leading to more fulfilling and authentic relationships.

What is your biggest takeaway?

....

....

....

....

5. Tackle a Tough Conversation

Having a tough conversation with someone who has a very different ID than you can be challenging, but it's possible to approach it in a constructive and respectful way. Here are some steps you can follow to tackle such a conversation effectively.

Self-reflection: Before engaging in the conversation, take some time for self-reflection. Understand your own ID and how it influences your perspective. This will help you approach the conversation with self-awareness and empathy.

Seek understanding: Begin the conversation by genuinely seeking to understand the other person's perspective. Listen actively and ask open-ended questions to encourage them to share their thoughts and motivations. Avoid judgment or interrupting. Try to see the situation from their point of view.

Empathize: Put yourself in the other person's shoes and try to empathize with their ID. Recognize that their values, experiences, and beliefs might be different from yours, and that doesn't make them wrong or inferior. Show empathy by acknowledging their feelings and validating their perspective.

Find common ground: Look for areas of common ground or shared values that can serve as a foundation for the conversation. Even if your IDs differ, there may still be underlying principles or goals that both of you can agree upon. Focus on those shared interests to build a bridge between your perspectives.

Communicate clearly and respectfully: Express your own thoughts and concerns clearly, using "I" statements to avoid sounding accusatory. Be respectful in your language and tone, ensuring that you don't belittle or dismiss the other person's perspective. Stay calm and composed, even if the conversation becomes heated.

Practice active listening: Active listening is crucial in tough conversations. Pay attention to both the words and the emotions behind them. Reflect back on what the other person has said to ensure you understood their perspective accurately. This demonstrates that you value their input and encourages them to do the same.

Find areas of compromise: Explore potential areas of compromise or solutions that can accommodate both perspectives. Be open to finding a middle ground or alternative approaches that satisfy the core needs of both parties. Collaboration and problem-solving should be the focus rather than trying to "win" the argument.

Remain open-minded: Remember that your ID is not the only valid perspective. Stay open-minded and be willing to challenge your own assumptions and beliefs. This will create an environment that encourages the other person to do the same, fostering mutual understanding and growth.

Agree to disagree: In some cases, it may not be possible to completely resolve the differences in IDs. Recognize that it's okay to disagree respectfully. Focus on maintaining a positive relationship despite the differences and acknowledge that different perspectives can coexist without causing harm.

Follow-up and reflect: After the conversation, take some time to reflect on what was discussed. Consider what you learned from the other person and how the conversation can help you grow. If appropriate, follow up with the person later to see if there are any further thoughts or actions to take.

> **TIP**
>
> Remember, tackling tough conversations requires patience, empathy, and a willingness to understand differing perspectives. By approaching the conversation with respect and openness, you can foster better communication and potentially find common ground.

What step will you take?

....

....

....

....

....

....

6. Circle of Control

You can link control, influence, and concern to the colors green, yellow, and red, respectively.

The center green can represent control because it symbolizes growth, stability, and harmony. When you have control over a situation, you can cultivate a sense of growth and stability, and create a harmonious environment where things run smoothly.

The middle yellow can represent influence because it symbolizes energy, optimism, and creativity. When you have influence, you can use your energy, optimism, and creativity to inspire others and shape their attitudes and behaviors towards a particular outcome.

The outer red can represent concern because it symbolizes passion, intensity, and urgency. When you are deeply concerned about something, you feel a sense of passion and intensity, and you may be motivated to take urgent action to ensure its success.

By using these colors to represent control, influence, and concern, you can create a visual shorthand for understanding and communicating these concepts. For example, if you are discussing a project and someone mentions that they have a lot of control over the outcome, you might visualize this as a green light, indicating that things are under control and moving forward smoothly. If someone else mentions that they are concerned about a particular aspect of the project, you might visualize this as a red light, indicating that urgent action may be needed to address the issue. And if someone else mentions that they are using their influence to motivate others towards a particular outcome, you might visualize this as a yellow light, indicating that they are using their energy and creativity to inspire others.

When dealing with someone who has a different ID than you and aiming to stay within your circle of control and circle of influence rather than the circle of concern, here are some strategies you can employ.

- Focus on your reactions: Instead of trying to change the other person's ID.
- Concentrate on managing your own responses and emotions.
- Recognize that you have control over how you react to situations and people and choose responses that align with your values and goals.

What is your action plan for moving forward? What do you need to be accountable for and what is in your circle of control? What do you need to let go?

This chapter on IDs for making meaningful connections has shed light on the intrinsic motivations and personal qualities that play a vital role in forming and nurturing meaningful relationships. Throughout this chapter, you have explored various factors such as empathy, authenticity, vulnerability, and active listening, which enable individuals to forge deep and lasting connections with others.

One key takeaway from this chapter is the recognition that meaningful connections are not solely reliant on external circumstances or chance encounters. Instead, they are rooted in the IDs that shape your attitudes and behaviors towards others. The cultivation of empathy allows you to understand and appreciate the perspectives of those around us, fostering a genuine sense of connection and mutual understanding.

Authenticity serves as a powerful catalyst for meaningful connections. By embracing your true self and expressing your thoughts and emotions honestly, you create an environment of trust and acceptance that encourages others to do the same. This authenticity also acts as a magnet, attracting individuals who resonate with your values and beliefs, leading to more meaningful and fulfilling relationships.

Summary

This chapter has also emphasized the importance of vulnerability in forming meaningful connections. Opening yourself up to others and being willing to share your fears, insecurities, and aspirations not only deepens the bond between individuals but also allows for a greater level of intimacy and emotional support.

Active listening has emerged as a crucial skill for making meaningful connections. By genuinely engaging in conversation and showing a sincere interest in others, you demonstrate your respect and value for their experiences and perspectives. This not only strengthens the connection but also fosters a deeper sense of mutual trust and understanding.

By focusing on Core-Connections and others IDs, you can increase self-awareness and intentional action in creating meaningful connections. By nurturing qualities such as empathy, authenticity, vulnerability, and active listening, you can forge deep and lasting relationships that bring fulfillment, support, and a sense of belonging. Ultimately, the cultivation of exploring others IDs enriches your life and allows you to create a more connected and empathetic relationships.

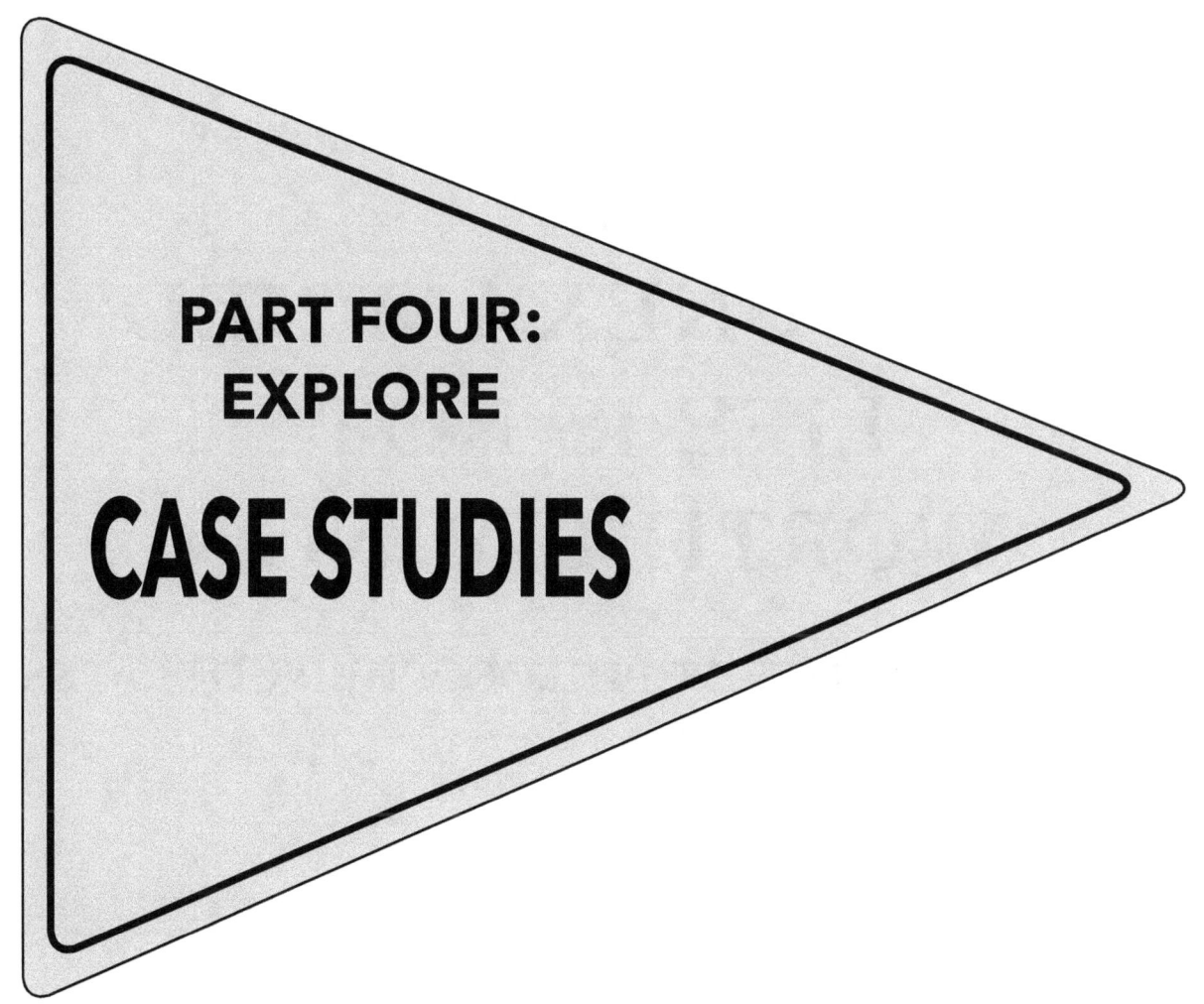

"The unexamined life is not worth living."

—Saying by Greek philosopher Socrates

CASE STUDIES

OFTEN IT IS helpful to read through Case Studies to better understand concepts. This part of the book is written to share real case studies from clients who have identified their ID and what they have learned from the experience.

Sarah's Quest for Self-Worth

INTRODUCTION
Sara is a 32-year-old marketing professional who works for a renowned advertising agency. Over the years, she has achieved considerable success in her career, but she is plagued by a deep-rooted need to prove her worth to herself and others. This case study will delve into Sara's background, explore the factors contributing to her ID, analyze its impact on her personal and professional lives, and suggest strategies for her to develop a healthier sense of self-worth.

Background

Sara grew up in a competitive environment where academic and extra-curricular achievements were highly valued. Her parents, both successful professionals, instilled in her the importance of excelling in all endeavors. While Sara was a high achiever, constantly receiving praise and recognition, she developed an unconscious belief that her worth was contingent on external validation.

Internal Driver

Sara's ID to prove her worth stems from a combination of factors. First, she harbors an intense fear of failure, fearing that any shortcomings or mistakes will undermine her sense of self-worth. Second, Sara experienced intermittent feelings of inadequacy throughout her childhood due to the high standards set by her parents and peers. Finally, her constant need for validation has become ingrained in her identity, leading her to rely on external achievements to feel validated and valued.

Impact on Personal Life

Sara 's drive to prove her worth has significantly impacted her personal life. She is constantly seeking approval from others, making it difficult for her to establish genuine connections and authentic relationships. Sara often feels intense pressure to meet expectations, resulting in anxiety, self-doubt, and a fear of rejection. This has led to a cycle of overworking, neglecting self-care, and sacrificing her personal needs and boundaries to maintain the appearance of success.

Impact on Professional Life

In her professional life, Sara 's ID has propelled her to achieve remarkable success. She consistently exceeds performance targets, receives accolades from clients and superiors, and is entrusted with high-profile projects. However, her relentless pursuit of external validation has led to burnout and an inability to find satisfaction in her accomplishments. She constantly fears being exposed as an impostor and worries that her worth is tied solely to her achievements, causing undue stress and self-imposed pressure.

STRATEGIES FOR DEVELOPMENT

Cultivating Self-Awareness: Sara could become aware of her patterns and the underlying beliefs driving her need for external validation. Through therapy, self-reflection, and mindfulness practices, she can uncover the root causes of her low self-worth and challenge the distorted beliefs that perpetuate it.

Redefining Success: Sara can explore alternative definitions of success beyond external achievements. By focusing on personal growth, self-compassion, and fulfilling relationships, she can develop a more holistic perspective of her worth, shifting the emphasis from external validation to internal contentment.

Celebrating Personal Achievements: Sara can learn to recognize and appreciate her personal achievements, regardless of their magnitude. By acknowledging her efforts, progress, and small victories, she can build a healthier sense of self-esteem that is not solely reliant on external recognition.

Establishing Boundaries: Sara can set boundaries in her personal and professional life to prioritize her well-being. By asserting herself, saying "no" when necessary, and allocating time for self-care and leisure activities, she can break free from the cycle of overworking and create a healthier work-life balance.

Seeking Support: Sara should seek support from loved ones, mentors, or a therapist who can provide guidance, reassurance, and perspective. Surrounding herself with a strong support system can help her challenge her self-defeating beliefs, provide encouragement, and foster a sense of belonging.

Conclusion

Sara's ID to prove her worth has both propelled her to professional success and caused significant personal distress. By undertaking the suggested strategies, Sara can embark on a journey of self-discovery, gradually freeing herself from the shackles of external validation and developing a healthier sense of self-worth based on intrinsic qualities and personal fulfillment.

Jake's Pursuit of Victory

Introduction

Jake is a 28-year-old competitive athlete who participates in various sports, including professional soccer and competitive martial arts. Throughout his life, he has displayed an intense internal drive to win in any endeavor he undertakes. This case study will explore Jake's background, examine the factors contributing to his ID, analyze its impact on his personal and professional life, and provide recommendations for developing a more balanced approach to competition.

Background

Jake grew up in a family that valued sports and encouraged him to participate in various competitive activities. From a young age, he exhibited exceptional athletic abilities and quickly discovered his passion for winning. The praise and recognition he received for his victories fueled his desire to excel and become the best in his chosen sports.

Internal Driver

Jake's ID to win is rooted in several factors. First, he possesses a strong competitive nature, always seeking new challenges and pushing himself to achieve victory. Second, he believes that winning validates his abilities and worth as an athlete. Third, Jake finds the thrill of competition exhilarating, and the desire to experience that euphoric feeling of success motivates him to push harder and strive for victory in every endeavor.

Impact on Personal Life

Jake's relentless drive to win has had a significant impact on his personal life. He often prioritizes his training and competitions over personal relationships, social activities, and self-care. This laser focus on victory has strained his relationships, as he may come across as overly competitive or neglectful of others' needs. Additionally, the pressure he places on himself to win can lead to high levels of stress, anxiety, and frustration when results do not meet his expectations.

Impact on Professional Life

In his professional athletic career, Jake's ID has propelled him to achieve remarkable success. He consistently outperforms his competitors, garners attention from sponsors and coaches, and has earned a reputation as a formidable athlete. However, this relentless pursuit of victory has the potential to lead to burnout, as Jake may sacrifice rest and recovery, overlook potential areas of improvement, and neglect long-term development in pursuit of immediate wins.

Strategies for Development

Redefining Success: Jake should consider broadening his definition of success beyond winning. By focusing on personal growth, skill development, and enjoying the process of competition, he can find fulfillment even in moments when victory eludes him. Emphasizing progress, resilience, and sportsmanship can help him develop a healthier perspective on success.

Balance and Self-Care: Jake needs to prioritize self-care and establish a balance between training, competition, and personal life. Incorporating rest, recovery, and leisure activities into his routine will help prevent burnout and enhance his overall performance. Building strong support networks, seeking social connection, and engaging in hobbies unrelated to his sport can provide a much-needed sense of balance.

Learning from Defeats: Jake should view defeats as opportunities for growth rather than personal failures. Analyzing his losses, identifying areas for improvement, and implementing changes in his training and strategies can help him become a more resilient and well-rounded athlete. A growth mindset will enable him to bounce back stronger from setbacks.

Sportsmanship and Collaboration: Encouraging a spirit of sportsmanship and collaboration with teammates and competitors can enhance Jake's overall experience in his sports. Celebrating others' victories, acknowledging their skills, and fostering positive relationships can create a more supportive and enjoyable environment, fostering personal growth and satisfaction.

Mental Skills Training: Jake could benefit from working with a sports psychologist or coach who specializes in mental skills training. Techniques such as visualization, goal setting, and mindfulness can help him manage his competitive drive, regulate his emotions, and maintain focus during competitions. Developing mental resilience and adopting a healthy perspective on winning can contribute to his long-term success and well-being.

Conclusion

Jake's Internal Drive to win has propelled him to achieve remarkable success in his athletic endeavors. However, it is essential for him to cultivate a more balanced and sustainable approach to competition. By redefining success, prioritizing self-care, learning from defeats, promoting sportsmanship, and developing mental skills, Jake can continue to pursue victory while also finding fulfillment, personal growth, and enjoyment in his chosen sports.

Emily's Need for Approval

Introduction

Emily is a 35-year-old professional working in a corporate setting. Throughout her life, she has demonstrated a strong internal drive to please others. This case study will delve into Emily's background, explore the factors contributing to her ID, analyze its impact on her personal and professional life, and propose strategies for developing a healthier sense of self and autonomy.

Background

Emily grew up in a family where meeting others' expectations was highly valued. As a child, she learned that receiving praise and approval from her parents and peers was essential for acceptance and love. Consequently, she developed an ID to please others, as it became ingrained in her identity and self-worth.

Internal Driver

Emily's internal driver to please stems from several factors. First, she has an innate desire for acceptance and approval from others, seeking validation as a source of self-esteem. Second, she experiences anxiety and discomfort when faced with potential disapproval or conflict, motivating her to avoid situations that may lead to disappointment or rejection. Finally, Emily may have learned that pleasing others is a reliable strategy for maintaining harmonious relationships, leading her to prioritize others' needs and desires over her own.

Impact on Personal Life

Emily's need to please others has had a significant impact on her personal life. She often prioritizes others' wants and needs at the expense of her own, neglecting self-care and personal boundaries. This can lead to a lack of fulfillment and a diminished sense of self. Additionally, her fear of disappointing others can result in difficulty making decisions, as she constantly seeks external validation and consensus from others. This may lead to a sense of powerlessness and a lack of assertiveness in personal relationships.

Impact on Professional Life

In her professional life, Emily's ID to please manifests as an over eagerness to please her superiors and colleagues. She frequently takes on additional work, accommodates unreasonable requests, and avoids conflict at all costs. While her dedication to others' satisfaction may be perceived positively, it can result in burnout, an imbalance of workload, and a lack of personal boundaries. Emily's inability to prioritize her own needs and assert herself may hinder her professional growth and limit her ability to advocate for herself.

Strategies for Development

Building Self-Awareness: Emily should focus on developing self-awareness regarding her patterns of people-pleasing. Recognizing her own needs, desires, and values will enable her to make conscious choices and establish a stronger sense of self.

Practicing Self-Validation: Emily should work on developing self-approval and self-validation. By acknowledging her own accomplishments, setting personal goals, and embracing self-compassion, she can reduce her reliance on external validation and build a stronger internal sense of worth.

Setting Healthy Boundaries: Emily needs to establish clear personal and professional boundaries. Learning to say "no" when necessary, delegating tasks, and asserting her needs will help her maintain a healthier work-life balance and prevent burnout.

Developing Assertiveness Skills: Emily should focus on building assertiveness skills, such as effective communication and conflict resolution techniques. Learning to express her opinions, set limits, and advocate for herself in a respectful manner will foster healthier relationships and increase her sense of empowerment.

Seeking Support: Emily can benefit from seeking support from a therapist or joining a support group. Professional guidance will help her explore the underlying reasons for her need to please others and develop strategies for building self-esteem, assertiveness, and self-advocacy.

Conclusion

Emily's ID to please others has had a significant impact on her personal and professional life. By developing self-awareness, practicing self-validation, setting healthy boundaries, developing assertiveness skills, and seeking support, Emily can work towards breaking the cycle of people-pleasing and cultivate a healthier sense of self. Ultimately, this will lead to increased personal fulfillment, improved relationships, and a greater sense of autonomy and self-worth.

Alex's Drive for Disruption

INTRODUCTION

Alex is a 29-year-old entrepreneur known for his relentless drive to disrupt established industries and challenge the status quo. This case study will explore Alex's background, examine the factors contributing to their ID for disruption, analyze its impact on his personal and professional life, and propose strategies for harnessing this drive in a positive and constructive manner.

BACKGROUND

Alex grew up in a family that encouraged independent thinking and questioning traditional norms. From an early age, he exhibited a natural inclination to challenge existing systems and explore alternative approaches. This mindset was further nurtured by exposure to innovative ideas and a supportive environment that embraced change.

INTERNAL DRIVER

Alex's ID for disruption is rooted in a combination of factors. First, they possess a strong desire to challenge the status quo and break free from the limitations of conventional thinking. Second, they are motivated by a deep-seated belief that innovation and progress are achieved through questioning and pushing boundaries. Third, Alex finds excitement and fulfillment in the process of creating something new and transformative.

IMPACT ON PERSONAL LIFE

Alex's drive for disruption significantly impacts their personal life. They often seek out unconventional experiences, relationships, and perspectives, which may lead to a sense of disconnection from more traditional social structures. Alex's propensity for change and exploration can also result in a lack of stability and consistency, making it challenging to maintain long-term personal commitments or find a sense of rootedness.

Impact on Professional Life

In their professional life, Alex's ID for disruption fuels their entrepreneurial pursuits. They are known for launching innovative ventures, challenging industry norms, and introducing groundbreaking ideas. While this drive can lead to significant successes and game-changing innovations, it can also present challenges. Alex may struggle with focusing on a single project or industry, often seeking new avenues for disruption. This can lead to a scattered approach and difficulty in achieving long-term stability and sustainable growth.

Strategies for Harnessing the Drive

Focus and Strategic Planning: Alex should consider channeling their drive for disruption by adopting a more focused and strategic approach. Identifying specific industries or areas where they can create meaningful change will allow for deeper impact and more sustainable ventures.

Collaboration and Partnerships: Building alliances with individuals who complement their skills and provide a balance of stability and continuity can help Alex bring their disruptive ideas to fruition. Collaborative partnerships can provide the structure and support needed to sustain and scale their ventures.

Research and Expertise: Deepening their understanding of the industries they aim to disrupt will enhance Alex's ability to identify gaps and create innovative solutions. Investing time in research, gaining industry-specific knowledge, and seeking mentorship or advisory roles can provide valuable insights and increase their chances of success.

Adaptability and Agility: Embracing adaptability and agility will enable Alex to navigate the uncertainties that come with disruption. Being open to feedback, adjusting strategies based on market dynamics, and rapidly iterating on ideas will help them stay ahead of the curve and maximize their impact.

Balancing Innovation with Sustainability: While disruption is often associated with rapid change, Alex should also consider the long-term sustainability and societal impact of their ventures. Incorporating ethical considerations, environmental responsibility, and social impact into their disruptive endeavors can ensure a more balanced and meaningful approach.

Conclusion

Alex's ID for disruption is a powerful force that can lead to transformative change and innovation. By harnessing this drive through focus, collaboration, research, adaptability, and a balanced approach to sustainability, Alex can achieve meaningful and lasting impact. Embracing the opportunities and challenges that come with disruption while maintaining a sense of purpose and responsibility will allow Alex to shape industries and create a positive legacy.

Alicia's Drive for Peacemaking

Introduction

Alicia is a 42-year-old individual who has consistently displayed a strong internal drive to be a peacemaker in various aspects of her life. This case study will delve into Alicia's background, explore the factors contributing to her ID for peacemaking, analyze its impact on her personal and professional life, and propose strategies for fostering constructive conflict resolution and maintaining personal well-being.

Background

Alicia grew up in a household where conflict resolution was highly valued, and peaceful communication was encouraged. From a young age, she observed the positive impact of peacemaking and developed a natural inclination towards seeking harmony and resolving conflicts. This upbringing has shaped her ID to be a peacemaker.

Internal Driver

Alicia's ID for peacemaking is rooted in several factors. First, she possesses a strong empathy and compassion for others, which motivates her to alleviate conflicts and create harmonious environments. Second, Alicia values open communication, seeking to create spaces where individuals can express their perspectives and concerns freely. Finally, she believes that peace and cooperation are essential for personal growth, well-being, and collective progress.

Impact on Personal Life

Alicia's drive for peacemaking significantly impacts her personal life. She invests time and energy in mediating conflicts among family members, friends, and acquaintances. While this drive fosters positive relationships and a sense of unity, Alicia may neglect her own needs and emotional well-being. The constant pursuit of peace can lead to emotional exhaustion and difficulty asserting her own boundaries or addressing personal conflicts.

Impact on Professional Life

In her professional life, Alicia's ID for peacemaking translates into her roles as a mediator, conflict resolution specialist, or team facilitator. She is highly valued for her ability to create a harmonious work environment and navigate conflicts effectively. However, Alicia may find it challenging to assert her own needs or engage in constructive confrontation when necessary. This can lead to an imbalance in power dynamics and hinder her professional growth.

Strategies for Development

Self-Care and Boundaries: Alicia should prioritize self-care and establish clear personal boundaries. Recognizing her own needs, practicing self-compassion, and setting limits on her involvement in conflicts will ensure that she maintains her emotional well-being while continuing to contribute to peacebuilding efforts.

Effective Communication: Alicia should focus on enhancing her communication skills, particularly in assertiveness and expressing her own needs and concerns. By developing effective communication techniques, she can contribute to conflict resolution while also ensuring her voice is heard and her own interests are addressed.

Conflict Transformation: Alicia can explore training and education in conflict transformation methodologies. These approaches focus on addressing the root causes of conflicts and fostering long-term sustainable solutions, enabling her to make a more profound impact in creating lasting peace.

Empowerment and Mediation: Alicia should consider empowering others to engage in conflict resolution and mediation themselves. By providing tools, education, and resources, she can create a culture of peace and equip individuals with the skills to address conflicts independently.

Collaboration and Partnerships: Alicia can strengthen her peacemaking efforts by collaborating with organizations and individuals dedicated to conflict resolution and peacebuilding. Engaging in networks, joining initiatives, and sharing experiences can expand her knowledge, resources, and impact.

Conclusion

Alicia's ID to be a peacemaker is a valuable asset that contributes to positive relationships and conflict resolution. By prioritizing self-care, developing effective communication skills, exploring conflict transformation methodologies, empowering others, and seeking collaboration, Alicia can enhance her peacemaking efforts while maintaining her own well-being. Balancing her drive for peace with self-advocacy and personal growth will enable her to make a lasting impact on individuals and communities, fostering a more harmonious and cooperative society.

Marks' Drive for Policing

Introduction

Mark is a 38-year-old individual who possesses a strong ID to police and enforce rules and regulations in various aspects of his life. This case study will delve into Mark's background, explore the factors contributing to his ID for policing, analyze its impact on his personal and professional life, and propose strategies for channeling this drive in a constructive and balanced manner.

Background

Mark's upbringing was characterized by a strong emphasis on discipline, structure, and adherence to rules. From a young age, he learned the importance of following established guidelines and felt a sense of responsibility to hold himself and others accountable. This upbringing shaped ID to police and enforce rules.

Internal Driver

Mark's ID for policing is influenced by several factors. Firstly, he values order and stability, believing that strict adherence to rules is essential for maintaining societal harmony. Secondly, he possesses a strong sense of justice and feels compelled to ensure fairness by upholding rules and regulations. Finally, Mark may have experienced situations where the consequences of rule-breaking were evident, reinforcing his drive to police and enforce standards.

Impact on Personal Life

Mark's drive for policing significantly impacts his personal life. He may find it challenging to relax and enjoy spontaneous or unstructured activities, as his focus is often on adhering to rules and maintaining order. This rigid mindset can limit his ability to adapt to change and embrace flexibility, potentially affecting personal relationships and overall life satisfaction.

Impact on Professional Life

In his professional life, Mark's IDs for policing may manifest in roles that involve law enforcement, compliance, or regulation. He is often recognized for his attention to detail, strong work ethic, and commitment to upholding standards. However, Mark's unwavering dedication to enforcing rules can sometimes create tension with colleagues or limit his ability to consider alternative approaches. This rigidity may hinder creativity and innovation within his professional endeavors.

Strategies for Development

Self-Reflection and Flexibility: Mark should engage in self-reflection to examine the underlying motivations behind his drive for policing. By cultivating an awareness of his own tendencies and embracing flexibility, he can challenge the rigidity of his mindset and explore alternative perspectives.

Empathy and Understanding: Developing empathy and understanding for others' perspectives can help Mark balance his drive for policing with compassion. This can enhance his ability to consider mitigating factors and context when assessing rule violations, fostering a more balanced and just approach.

Collaborative Problem-Solving: Mark should embrace a collaborative approach to problem-solving, seeking input from others and engaging in dialogue when addressing rule violations or non-compliance. By involving stakeholders in decision-making processes, he can create a sense of shared responsibility and promote a more inclusive and participatory environment.

Leadership and mentoring: Mark can use his drive for policing in a positive manner by mentoring others and providing guidance on rules and regulations. This allows him to share his expertise and knowledge while empowering others to understand and follow established guidelines.

Personal Growth and Work-Life Balance: Mark should prioritize personal growth and work-life balance to ensure a well-rounded life. Engaging in hobbies, pursuing interests outside of work, and developing relationships beyond rule enforcement can contribute to his overall fulfillment and reduce the risk of burnout.

Conclusion

Mark's ID to police and enforce rules can be a valuable asset when balanced with flexibility, empathy, and collaborative problem-solving. By engaging in self-reflection, fostering empathy, adopting a collaborative approach, embracing leadership and mentoring, and prioritizing personal growth and work-life balance, Mark can channel his drive in a constructive and balanced manner. This will allow him to make a positive impact on rule compliance while fostering understanding, fairness, and adaptability in both his personal and professional life.

Jessica's Drive to Prove a Point

Introduction

Jessica is a 31-year-old individual who possesses a strong Internal Drive to prove a point in various aspects of her life. This case study will explore Jessica's background, examine the factors contributing to her ID to prove a point, analyze its impact on her personal and professional life, and propose strategies for channeling this drive in a constructive and effective manner.

Background

Jessica grew up in an environment where critical thinking and expressing opinions were highly valued. From an early age, she developed a keen sense of observation and analysis, coupled with a strong desire to challenge existing beliefs and assumptions. This upbringing influenced her ID to prove a point and seek validation for her perspectives.

Internal Driver

Jessica's ID to prove a point is influenced by several factors. Firstly, she possesses a natural curiosity and intellectual thirst for knowledge, leading her to question prevailing narratives and seek alternative viewpoints. Secondly, Jessica has a strong need for validation and recognition, and proving her point serves as a means to establish her credibility and worth. Finally, she may have had experiences where her opinions were dismissed or overlooked, further fueling her drive to assert herself and validate her ideas.

Impact on Personal Life

Jessica's drive to prove a point significantly impacts her personal life. She may engage in frequent debates and discussions, seeking opportunities to challenge prevailing opinions and express her own perspectives. This can lead to strained relationships or social dynamics, as others may perceive her as argumentative or confrontational. Jessica's strong need for validation may also create emotional distress if her viewpoints are not acknowledged or respected.

Impact on Professional Life

In her professional life, Jessica's ID to prove a point may manifest as a drive for success and recognition. She seeks opportunities to showcase her expertise and ideas, often taking on challenging projects or assuming leadership roles. While this drive can lead to achievements and innovation, Jessica may encounter resistance from colleagues or face difficulties in collaborating if she becomes overly focused on proving her point rather than considering alternative perspectives.

Strategies for Development

Active Listening and Empathy: Jessica should cultivate active listening skills and empathy to better understand others' perspectives. This allows her to engage in meaningful dialogue, consider different viewpoints, and establish rapport with others, fostering more constructive and collaborative conversations.

Balanced Approach: Jessica should strive for a balanced approach in proving her point. While it is important to assert her opinions, she should also be open to feedback and acknowledge the value of diverse perspectives. Finding common ground and seeking mutually beneficial solutions can enhance her ability to influence others positively.

Research and Evidence-Based Arguments: Jessica can strengthen her ability to prove her point by conducting thorough research and relying on evidence-based arguments. This ensures that her assertions are well-informed, credible, and persuasive, increasing the likelihood of her ideas being accepted and respected by others.

Relationship Building and Collaboration: Jessica should prioritize relationship building and collaboration. Building strong connections with colleagues and stakeholders can create a supportive environment where her ideas are more readily accepted. Collaboration also enables her to leverage diverse expertise, leading to more robust and well-rounded solutions.

Managing Emotions and Recognizing Limits: Jessica should be mindful of her emotional reactions and impulses when engaging in discussions or debates. Recognizing her limits and knowing when to step back or take a break can prevent conflicts and maintain a healthy work-life balance.

Conclusion

Jessica's ID to prove a point can be a valuable asset when channeled effectively. By cultivating active listening skills, embracing empathy, adopting a balanced approach, relying on research and evidence, prioritizing relationship building and collaboration, and managing emotions, Jessica can engage in constructive dialogue, positively influence others, and foster an environment of open-mindedness and growth. This will allow her to validate her ideas while maintaining strong relationships and achieving success both personally and professionally.

Ethan's Drive to be the Real Deal

Introduction

Ethan is a 35-year-old individual who possesses a strong internal drive to be the real deal in various aspects of his life. This case study will explore Ethan's background, examine the factors contributing to his ID to be the real deal, analyze its impact on his personal and professional life, and propose strategies for channeling this drive in a positive and authentic manner.

Background

Ethan grew up in an environment that emphasized the importance of authenticity and integrity. From an early age, he witnessed the impact of genuine individuals who remained true to their values and principles. This upbringing shaped Ethan's ID to be the real deal and prioritize authenticity in his actions and interactions.

Ethan's ID to be the real deal is influenced by several factors. Firstly, he values personal integrity and authenticity, believing that genuine actions and intentions are essential for building trust and meaningful connections. Secondly, Ethan has a deep desire to make a positive impact on others and seeks to be a role model by exemplifying authenticity in his behavior. Finally, he may have experienced situations where he witnessed the consequences of deception or inauthenticity, further fueling his drive to be the real deal.

Impact on Personal Life

Ethan's drive to be the real deal significantly impacts his personal life. He strives to align his words and actions with his values, which contributes to a strong sense of self and personal fulfillment. Ethan's authenticity allows him to attract like-minded individuals and build deep, meaningful relationships. However, his commitment to being genuine may also make it challenging for him to navigate situations where compromise or diplomacy is required, potentially leading to conflicts or strained relationships.

Impact on Professional Life

In his professional life, Ethan's ID to be the real deal translates into a strong work ethic, commitment to quality, and a focus on delivering genuine value. He is highly regarded for his authenticity, transparency, and the trust he engenders in colleagues and clients. However, Ethan's unwavering commitment to authenticity may result in a higher degree of risk aversion, making it challenging for him to step outside his comfort zone or embrace innovation.

Strategies for Development

Self-Reflection and Values Clarification: Ethan should engage in self-reflection and clarify his core values to ensure that his actions align with his authentic self. This will provide a solid foundation for decision-making and enable him to navigate situations where compromise or adaptation is necessary without sacrificing his integrity.

Emotional Intelligence and Empathy: Developing emotional intelligence and empathy can help Ethan understand and connect with others on a deeper level. This will enable him to balance his authenticity with an understanding of different perspectives, enhancing his ability to collaborate and build effective relationships.

Growth Mindset and Adaptability: Ethan should embrace a growth mindset and cultivate adaptability to navigate new challenges and opportunities. This will allow him to explore innovative approaches while maintaining his authenticity, fostering personal and professional growth.

Courageous Vulnerability: Ethan can practice courageous vulnerability by openly sharing his thoughts, feelings, and experiences, even when they are uncomfortable. This fosters trust and creates an environment where others feel safe to be authentic as well, promoting deeper connections and collaboration.

Continuous Learning and Feedback: Ethan should prioritize continuous learning and seek feedback from trusted individuals. This will allow him to refine his authenticity and expand his perspectives, leading to personal and professional growth.

Conclusion

Ethan's internal drive to be the real deal is a powerful motivator for personal and professional growth. By engaging in self-reflection, clarifying values, developing emotional intelligence and empathy, embracing a growth mindset, practicing courageous vulnerability, and pursuing continuous learning, Ethan can channel his drive in a positive and authentic manner. This will enable him to make a genuine impact on others, foster meaningful connections, and navigate challenges with integrity and adaptability.

Pam's Drive to be Relevant

INTRODUCTION

Pam is a 42-year-old individual who possesses a strong internal drive to be relevant in various aspects of her life. This case study will delve into Pam's background, examine the factors contributing to her ID to be relevant, analyze its impact on her personal and professional life, and propose strategies for channeling this drive in a healthy and balanced manner.

BACKGROUND

Pam grew up in a fast-paced and competitive environment where staying up-to-date and being in the know was highly valued. From an early age, she learned the importance of keeping trends, advancements, and knowledge. This upbringing shaped Pam's ID to be relevant and be seen as someone who is knowledgeable and up-to-date.

Pam's goal to be relevant is influenced by several factors. Firstly, she values the ability to contribute meaningfully to conversations and projects, believing that staying relevant is essential for credibility and influence. Secondly, Pam has a fear of being left behind or overlooked, which drives her to continuously seek new information and skills. Finally, she may have experienced instances where her lack of relevance hindered her opportunities or recognition, further fueling her drive to be relevant.

IMPACT ON PERSONAL LIFE

Pam's drive to be relevant significantly impacts her personal life. She invests considerable time and effort in staying informed and up-to-date, often participating in various activities, courses, and events. While this drive allows her to engage in meaningful conversations and expand her knowledge, it may also create a sense of pressure or overwhelm. Pam's focus on being relevant can sometimes overshadow other aspects of her life, such as personal relationships or self-care.

Impact on Professional Life

In her professional life, Pam's ID to be relevant translates into a strong work ethic and commitment to professional growth. She actively seeks opportunities to learn and develop new skills, positioning herself as an expert in her field. Pam's relevance and knowledge contribute to her professional success and recognition. However, her relentless pursuit of relevance may lead to workaholism or difficulties in balancing work and personal life.

Strategies for Development

Purposeful Relevance: Pam should focus on being relevant in areas aligned with her passions, interests, and goals. This ensures that her efforts to stay relevant are purposeful and meaningful, allowing her to invest time and energy in areas that truly matter to her.

Continuous Learning with Balance: Pam should prioritize continuous learning while maintaining a healthy work-life balance. Setting boundaries and allocating time for personal activities and relationships will help prevent burnout and ensure a more well-rounded life.

Selective Information Consumption: Pam should adopt a selective approach to information consumption. Rather than trying to keep up with everything, she can focus on a few key areas of interest or relevance to deepen her knowledge and expertise.

Networking and Collaboration: Pam should actively engage in networking and collaboration opportunities. Building connections with individuals who share similar interests or professional goals can foster mutually beneficial relationships and expand her sphere of relevance.

Reflection and Self-Assessment: Pam should periodically reflect on her ID for relevance and assess if it aligns with her values and overall well-being. Engaging in self-assessment exercises and seeking feedback from trusted individuals can provide valuable insights and help recalibrate her priorities.

Conclusion

Pam's Internal Drive to be relevant can be a powerful motivator for personal and professional growth. By focusing on purposeful relevance, maintaining a healthy balance, adopting a selective approach to information consumption, engaging in networking and collaboration, and periodically reflecting on her priorities, Pam can channel her drive in a healthy and balanced manner. This will allow her to stay informed and engaged while also prioritizing personal well-being, meaningful relationships, and a fulfilling life beyond the pursuit of relevance.

ABC's for Success: Awareness, Behaviors, Connections

Your Case Study

INTRODUCTION

BACKGROUND

INTERNAL DRIVER

IMPACT ON PERSONAL LIFE

IMPACT ON PROFESSIONAL LIFE

STRATEGIES FOR DEVELOPMENT

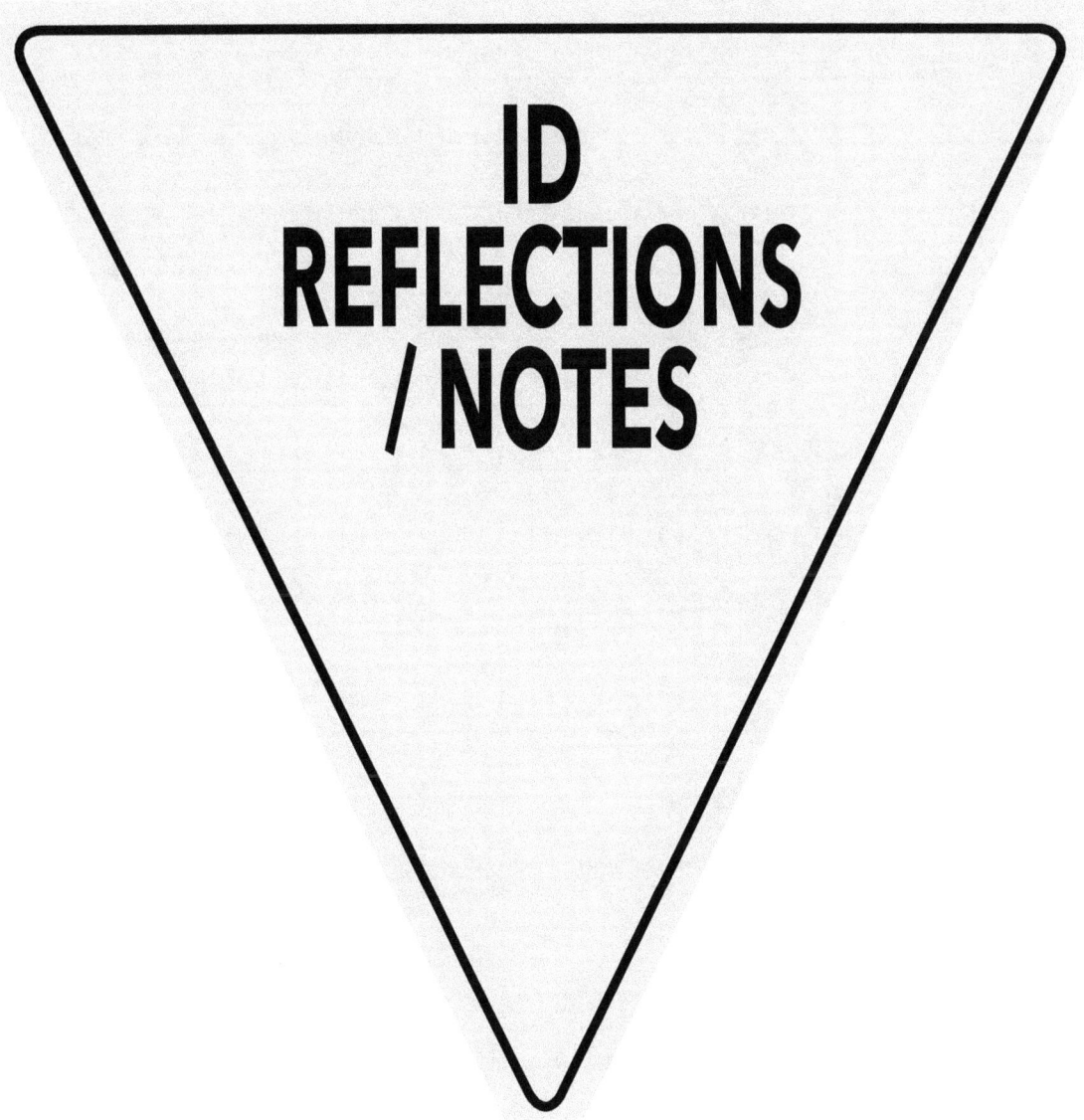

ID Reflections/Notes

ID Reflections/Notes

ID Reflections/Notes

ID Reflections/Notes

ID Reflections/Notes

ID Reflections/Notes

ID Reflections/Notes

ID Reflections/Notes

ID Reflections/Notes

ID Reflections/Notes

ID Reflections/Notes

ID Reflections/Notes

ID Reflections/Notes

ID Reflections/Notes

ID Reflections/Notes

ID Reflections/Notes

ID Reflections/Notes

ID Reflections/Notes

ID Reflections/Notes

ID Reflections/Notes

ABOUT THE AUTHOR

JENN CHLOUPEK HAS been igniting, transforming, and empowering success for 25 remarkable years. She is a seasoned educator, prolific author, adept facilitator, and a revered Master Executive coach whose indelible impact spans a remarkable quarter-century. With an unwavering dedication to unlocking human potential, Jenn has left an indelible mark on the worlds of corporate powerhouses and federal agencies alike.

For two and a half decades, Jenn's dynamic teaching methods have shaped countless minds, instilling a thirst for knowledge and growth. Her profound insights have not only enriched classrooms but have radiated throughout boardrooms, creating a lasting legacy of wisdom.

As a wordsmith of unparalleled finesse, Jenn has penned literary creations that transcend mere books, becoming guides to transformation. Her written works are cherished beacons, illuminating paths to success, personal empowerment, and holistic well-being.

With an innate ability to harness collective energy, Jenn has orchestrated transformative workshops, enabling groups to unite their potential and achieve unprecedented heights. Her facilitation prowess turns challenges into stepping stones and complexities into opportunities.

Jenn's mastery as an Executive Coach has propelled individuals and organizations towards excellence. She doesn't just guide; she empowers leaders to uncover their latent capacities, fostering growth that resonates across professional landscapes.

Her mission transcends the ordinary; she's dedicated to knitting together the fabric of human connection. Be it connecting individuals to themselves, linking them with invaluable tools and resources, or forging bonds between kindred spirits, her influence radiates through every connection she nurtures.

Nestled amidst the picturesque landscapes of Arizona, Jenn calls this haven home. Alongside her devoted husband Lar, she's embarked on her own adventure, a parallel journey of love, laughter, and shared dreams. Her nurturing spirit extends to her cherished family. As a proud mother to two sons, Jacob and Colton, and a devoted dog mom to Chase, she exemplifies the essence of devotion and nurturing.

www.ingramcontent.com/pod-product-compliance
Lightning Source LLC
Chambersburg PA
CBHW060344010526
44117CB00017B/2960